Francis Alexander Durivage

The Glenaloon and Other Poems

Francis Alexander Durivage

The Glenaloon and Other Poems

ISBN/EAN: 9783744709828

Printed in Europe, USA, Canada, Australia, Japan

Cover: Foto ©Thomas Meinert / pixelio.de

More available books at **www.hansebooks.com**

Entirely Yours

F. A. Durivage

AND

OTHER POEMS.

BY

FRANCIS A. DURIVAGE.

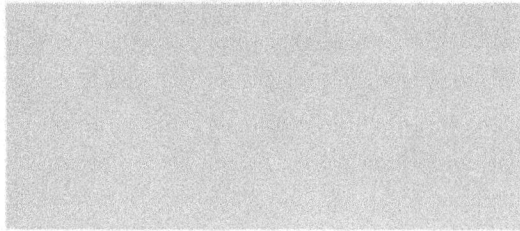

NEW YORK:
TROW'S PRINTING AND BOOKBINDING CO.,
201–213 EAST TWELFTH STREET,
1881.

Trow's
Printing and Bookbinding Company,
201–213 East 12th Street,
New York.

Dedication.

TO THOSE WHO REMEMBER

MR. DURIVAGE,

MANY OF THEM HIS LIFE-LONG FRIENDS,

THIS VOLUME OF HIS POEMS IS DEDICATED,

BY HIS DAUGHTER,

M. RITCHIE DURIVAGE BENNETT.

CONTENTS.

viii   *Contents.*

FRANCIS ALEXANDER DURIVAGE.

A BIOGRAPHICAL SKETCH.

BY W. S. CHASE.

SHALL a man devote himself exclusively to literature, or shall he pursue some trade or profession
as an ἔργον, a business, and literature as a πάρεργον, an
accessory or mere by-business? The discussion of this
question by Coleridge and De Quincey led those writers
from their different points of view to diametrically opposite conclusions. Coleridge solemnly adjured the
aspirant to literary distinction—"Never pursue literature as a trade!" while De Quincey as solemnly de-
clared one point to be clear to his judgment—"that
literature must decay, unless we have a class wholly
dedicated to that service, not pursuing it as an amusement, only with weary and pre-occupied minds." Here,
as in most cases, the truth of the matter probably lies
somewhere between extreme opinions on both sides. As
one result of future experiments in organizing American
society, it may be found worth more than it will cost to
spare out of our overstocked trades and professions and
to completely equip and adequately compensate men
enough to compose, as De Quincey suggests, a garrison

*1

on permanent duty for the service of the highest pur-
poses which grace and dignify our nature.   It will then
be manifest that singleness of aim is no less indispen-
sable to excellence and success in literature than in any
other line of human effort.   Even now the volunteer in
the noble service of literature must give himself up to it
without reserve or limitation—he enlists "for the war"
and can count on no furlough.   But in order to serve
efficiently he must have an income sufficient to feed,
clothe, and shelter him and those dependent on him, and
fully to arm and equip him for his chosen work.   To be
sane, sound, and happy let him derive such an income
from some ἔργον, a regular employment which does not
depend on the will of the moment, and which can be
carried on so far mechanically that an average quantum
only of health, spirits, and intellectual exertion is requisite to its faithful discharge.   He may then hope to res-
cue from a few evenings, or mornings, the leisure need-
ful and sufficient for a larger product in literature of
what is truly genial than would be yielded by whole
days and weeks of compulsory authorship.

The late Francis Alexander Durivage was, during the
greater part of his life, a signal example of the advan-
tages of having both an ἔργον and a πάρεργον, and of
complying faithfully with the demands of each.   It is at
once a lesson and an encouragement to find how much
he was able to do in the way of self-culture, mental dis-
cipline, the acquisition of knowledge, and the development of exceptional talents as a writer of prose and
verse, and as a draughtsman and painter.   What admir-

able use he made of unusual gifts, accomplishments, and
opportunities ! How creditable, both in quantity and
quality, **was** the literary and artistic work achieved by
him in addition to the honest and satisfactory discharge
of his duties as a Government official, as a private citizen, as neighbor, **friend,** husband, **and father !** As a
journalist he fortunately **was never exposed to being
hampered and** humiliated **by** any expectation (impossi-
ble in his case) **that he** might become either a mere
mouthpiece of some stupid and pompous political boss,
or a mere amanuensis of some rich ignoramus, who fancies that a supply of brains can be bought cheap for
cash, and that a newspaper, **like** a paper-mill, **or rum-**
mill, **or** any mill, is **to** be run solely to make money **or**
to further other selfish interests. Although a **frequent**
and copious writer for magazines as well **as** newspapers,
Mr. Durivage wholly escaped the wretchedness depicted
with such forcible truth by Talfourd as "the lot of those
self-fancied poets and panting essayists who live on from
volume **to** volume, or from magazine to magazine, who
tremble with nervous delight **at a** favorable mention, are ·
cast down by **a** sly alliteration **or** satirical play on their
names, and die of an elaborate **eulogy"** in aromatic
pain. They **live** in the lying breath of contemporary
report, and bask out a sort of occasional holiday in the
glimmer of public favor. They are always in a feverish
struggle, yet they make no progress. There is no dra-
matic coherence, no unity **of action in the** tragi-comedy
of their **lives.** They **have hits and** brilliant passages,
perhaps, which **may come on review** before them in

straggling succession; but nothing dignified or massive, tending **to** one end of good **or** evil. **They begin** life once a quarter, or **once a** month, according to the will of their publishers. They dedicate nothing to posterity; but toil on for applause till praise sickens, and their "life's idle business" grows too heavy to be borne. They give their thoughts immaturely to the world, and thus spoil **them for** themselves forever. Their own earliest and deepest and most sacred feelings become at last dull commonplaces, which they have talked of and written about until they are glad to escape from the theme. Their days are not "linked each **to each by natural piety**," but at best bound together in forgotten volumes. Better, far better than this, is the lot of those whose characters and pretensions have little "mark of likelihood," whose days are filled **up** by the exercises of honest industry, and who, on looking back, recognize their lives **only by the turns** of their fortune, or the events which **have called forth their** affections." Of such is the kingdom of everyday real life—often stranger and of **more** thrilling **interest** than fiction—and **over** which George Eliot, the greatest of modern novelists, wisely chose to reign, contentedly hiding therein her own splendid individuality and selecting therefrom her favorite heroines and heroes. Among the latter Durivage was well worthy to stand, for, voluntarily chaining himself to the wheel **of** everyday life, he resisted all temptation to the extravagances of thought and action which too often lead the ill-regulated genius astray; and his constancy in ever doing "the duty that lies nearest" gave solidity to floating minutes, hours, and days, putting into his life the harmony, the proportion that belongs pre-eminently to the lives of those, happiest of all, who, with one great aim, with one idea of practical or visionary good to which they are wedded, devote **their** undivided energy **to a single pursuit.**

Francis **Alexander Durivage was born at Boston, Massachusetts, on April 7,** 1814, in the midst **of the second war of the United States for** independence. The stirring incidents of that war (1812–1814), the struggle of the South American republics against Spanish misrule (1810–1819), and that of Greece against Turkish despotism (1822–1829), the downfall of Napoleon I., Emperor of the French, his sudden return from the island of Elba (March **1,** 1815), his brief restoration of the empire, and **his final** defeat at the battle of Waterloo (June 18, **1815), and** the French Revolution of 1830, were among events **nearly** synchronous with the period that covered the infancy and youth of Durivage. He was about ten years of age when Lafayette, the friend and companion-in-arms of Washington, revisited the United States, and everywhere revived the memories of our first war for independence. The illustrious French General met with no heartier welcome than the famous apostrophe with which Edward Everett concluded his oration before the Phi-Beta-Kappa Society of Harvard College, at Cambridge, Massachusetts, in 1824, an oration which will always remain a **model of A**merican eloquence. Durivage, **boy as** he was at the **time of Lafayette's** memorable **visit to America in** 1824, shared the more fully in the enthusiasm awakened by the nation's guest, from the fact that his own paternal grandfather, was, like Lafayette, a Frenchman of noble descent. This grandfather, a scion of an ancient family in Brittany, the Caillauds, whose ancestral honors dated from before the first Crusade (ending in 1099), came to New England from the island of Martinique, which was discovered by Christopher Columbus in 1502 and settled by French colonists from St. Christopher's in 1635. In New England and in Martinique he adopted the surname of Du Rivage, a territorial name of the Caillauds, and his gravestone in a churchyard at New London, Conn., bears this inscription, " François Nicolas Caillaud Durivage. Died October 5, 1794, Aged 51 years." His son, Francis Shute Durivage, for many years a merchant, and also well known as a professor of painting and the French language, in Boston, Massachusetts, married in that city a lady of rare worth and intelligence, the sister of Alexander and Edward Everett, both of whom became eminent orators, statesmen, and diplomatists. The former, before being United States Minister to China, was President of the University of Louisiana, and the latter, after being United States Minister to England, was President of Harvard University, and, during the memorable Presidential campaign of 1860, he was the candidate of the Bell and Everett party for the Vice-Presidency of the nation. In 1861 Mr. Francis A. Durivage became the private secretary of his Uncle Edward, and gladly improved opportunities for discovering how much more warmth of heart as well as intellectual vigor and substantial learning than the world generally knew abounded beneath the dignified and apparently cold exterior of the celebrated orator.

If the late **Mr.** George Ripley had **lived** to complete his projected " History of Boston Culture," he could not have omitted as one of **its** chief **elements the** influence of more than one **family, which, like the Everett** family, united **the best European and American characteristics of** home **life, that bright** consummate **flower of** modern **civilization. In** such **a family** Francis Durivage was born and nurtured. **He** grew up a true Boston boy, but it would be interesting and suggestive to trace how Boston surroundings affected without changing the essentially French texture and color of **his mind** and temperament. Schoolmates are often formed and **instructed as much by each other** as by their preceptors, and at the **Latin** school which Francis early entered he was educated **and** taught **not** only by the best teachers of the day, **but also** by close companionship with bright and studious lads, many of whom subsequently became distinguished men, **as,** for instance, George S. Hillard, Charles Sumner, Oliver Wendell Holmes, and John Fitzpatrick (afterward, as Bishop **of** Boston, a worthy successor of Cardinal Cheverus). With several of these early associates he was united by ties of mutual friendship throughout life. I have heard more than one of them, and especially Bishop Fitzpatrick, speak most affectionately of him and **of** the fair blossoms which in the springtide of his life promised **a rich** and fruitful manhood. His talents and character had **been** quickened to an almost precocious development, and even while a school-boy he gave signs of an extraordinary vocation for literature. Without neglecting at all his regular studies, he was an omniverous reader of the best miscellaneous English and French books, with not a few of which he first became familiar by stealth, as it were, behind a rampart of dictionaries piled up on his desk at the Latin school. When twelve or thirteen years old he wrote, in prose and in verse, many " pieces" that were " spoken " on public occasions by his schoolmates, and several of these productions found their way into print in the journals of Boston and other cities. At sixteen years of age he became himself an editor, and brought out a weekly paper, the *Amateur*, among the contributors to which were names of brilliant promise since amply fulfilled. It was for the *Amateur* that the future " Autocrat of the Breakfast-table," Oliver Wendell Holmes, wrote his earliest poem, " The Last Leaf." At the age of fourteen Durivage had already begun to write professedly for the press, and for many years he was a regular contributor to the *New York Mirror*, the *Spirit of the Times*, and the *Knickerbocker Magazine*, and, subsequently, to the *Atlantic Monthly*, and to the *Old and New*, which was so ably edited by his cousin, Rev. Edward Everett Hale, who, amidst his apostolical labors as preacher and pastor, somehow finds time also for a great amount and variety of first-class literary work. Not long after Mr. Durivage fairly commenced his journalistic career, he attracted the attention of S. G. Goodrich (so well known as Peter Parley), who hastened to impress him into the useful and honorable service in which he deserves the credit of having been himself a pioneer, that of combining entertainment and instruction in books for juvenile readers.

Peter Parley is said to have shrewdly exploited to his own fame and profit a number of *collaborateurs*, whose talents he claimed to have first discovered and made known to the world. Conspicuous among these were Nathaniel Hawthorne, N. P. Willis, Madame Calderon de la Barca, and F. A. Durivage. The last-named was the "working editor" through many volumes of *Peter Parley's Magazine*, which long enjoyed a large circulation among the youth of America and Great Britain. He was justly permitted to put his own name on the title-page of the "Cyclopædia of History," one of the most careful and extensive of the compilations contributed by him to Peter Parley's works (so-called). While toiling industriously as an assistant of S. G. Goodrich, Durivage also contributed largely to Buckingham's *New England Magazine*, then flourishing under the editorship of Park Benjamin. In 1840, Simeon Borden, the State Engineer, engaged him as draughtsman to prepare for the engraver the Map of Massachusetts. To reduce to order and beauty a maze of topographical lines and of lettering on a sheet of paper six feet by four was no slight task ; but Mr. Durivage did it perfectly, in exact imitation of copper-plate. He soon afterward joined the editorial staff of the *Boston Daily Times*, at the head of which he long remained. He, moreover, edited for several years *The Yankee Blade*. He succeeded Mr. E. H. Chapin as editor of *The Symbol and Odd Fellows' Magazine*, and he was editorially connected with *The Olive Branch*, and other Boston publi-

cations, precursors in New England of Bonner's *New
York Ledger* and Street and Smith's *New York Weekly*,
which have had such an immense circulation in the Mid-
dle, Western, and Southern States, and to which, also,
at a later period, he was a frequent and copious contributor. Whatever complaints over-fastidious, carping critics
may allege against weekly newspapers which have been
so prodigiously successful with the masses of the people,
no historian of the intellectual progress of America can
overlook their importance, if only in having diffused a
vast amount of information, and in having awakened a
taste and habit of reading, the consequences of which
are incalculable. Nor can it be denied that these and
similar publications have largely helped in preparing the
public mind for that " blessed ministry of books " which
Durivage fully enjoyed and valued, "and which," as a
wise old writer says, "cannot be too much extolled."
Durivage and his fellow-workers in this wide field de-
served well of the republic, not only by sowing in it with
seed for harvest, to be reaped by countless minds, but
also by fortifying it against all encroachments of immoral-
ity. Intellectually, no less than morally, the high standard
of morality exacted of the popular fireside newspapers in
the United States is of inestimable advantage.

Durivage is likewise entitled to a no less inconsiderable
share of whatever credit is due to the prodigious development and beneficial influences of illustrated periodical
literature in the United States. He was for nine years
associate editor of the first pictorial newspaper published
in America, not only supplying much of its letter-press,

but himself contributing **to its** illustrated department
many architectural and other designs, which he drew on
wood for the engravers. When Mr. M. M. Ballou, the well-
known writer and publisher, purchased *Gleason's Pictorial*, **Mr.** Durivage became assistant editor of *Ballou's
Pictorial* and *The Flag of Our Union*, **contributing to**
them poems, essays, **comic sketches, novelettes, and oc-
casionally art illustrations. The relations between Mr.
Ballou and his life-long friend, Mr.** Durivage, happily
illustrated the possibility of realizing, even before the
millennium, an ideal, seldom enough realized, of the potential relations between publisher and editor, who are
usually defined as natural enemies. While I had editorial
charge of *Frank Leslie's Illustrated Newspaper*, at a
much later period, both the late Mr. Leslie and **I were**
glad to count upon **Mr.** Durivage as an occasional **con-**
tributor and an ever-judicious adviser. A pamphlet might
be filled with the full list of periodicals, illustrated or not
illustrated, to which Mr. Durivage was, at various times,
a frequent and welcome contributor. Many bulky volumes would be required to contain the innumerable
"articles" which indicated his seemingly exhaustless
mental resources **and** almost incredible literary facility,
and which proved him to be equally successful as a *racon-
teur*, a reviewer, an art-critic, **a** writer of political "leaders," or a terse, pungent paragrapher. Under his signature
of "The Old 'Un," he won a popularity as speedy and
as universal as that of any of the **legion of "**American
Humorists" who have **since followed in his** footsteps. It
may safely **be** added **that few** of them have yet overtaken

him, and none have surpassed him in blending both wit
and humor in exhibitions of the comic phases of American
life. In 1848 Mr. Durivage and his friend, Capt. Burnham, collected their fugitive sketches of humorous
characters, most of which had appeared in Porter's *Spirit
of the Times,* into a volume, which was published by
Carey & Hart, of Philadelphia, with the title of "Stray
Subjects, by the Old 'Un and the Young 'Un." This
volume was embellished with illustrations by Darley, and
it had a large sale. In 1854 similar success attended
the publication of a selection from Mr. Durivage's graver
writings, with the title of "Life Scenes Sketched in
Light and Shadow." In 1849, Phillips, Samson & Co.
published the first American edition of Lamartine's " History of the French Revolution of 1848 ; Translated by
Francis A. Durivage and William S. Chase." This translation, or at least his share of it, attested the rare capacity
of Mr. Durivage for uniting speed with excellence in
literary work (it was achieved in an unprecedentedly short
time, during hours snatched from sleep and a pressure
of work of another kind) and his mastery of the difficult
art of a translator. "A conscientious translator is perpetu-
ally drawn in opposite directions from the wish to accom-
plish two incompatible objects—to give an exact representation of his original, and, at the same time, to make
that representation an idiomatic one." Durivage, in
translating from French, Spanish, Italian, or German,
always observed the rules laid down and so well exemplified by the poet Percival, who said, " My first principle
is that the version be *recht treu ;* my second, that it be

recht gut: that is, I had rather it be strictly faithful, though a little inferior in composition, than that it be perfect as a composition, yet unfaithful to the original." The numerous translations with which Mr. Durivage enriched the English language are equally true and good. He was one of the best and most **faithful of translators.**

As an original **writer he signally illustrated** the **fact** that "only when a man's thoughts issue from his own head and heart, can they come forth ready clad in the fittest words."** He **usually** wrote with the spontaneity and ease with which the Italian *improvisatore* recites. Yet if he ever verged upon a dangerous facility he was protected from falling into faults, which might otherwise have **been** inevitable, by holding in mind, even on **trivial occasions, a** constant sense of those classical **models of** style which he had studied early and late until **they had become part and** parcel of his intellectual being. **True to his** French origin, he deemed clearness and direct**ness** the chief merits **of** composition ; **and in** order to attain these merits, he willingly rejected whatever Horace could have **condemned as "purple** patchwork tagged on to make a great show." Yea, few **writers** have had **at** command a richer vocabulary, English and foreign, or **a** greater store of poetical imagery, than he. He was fond of quoting with approval what Niebuhr said to Lieber : "Persons who have never tried to write at once cor**rectly, do** not know how easy it is, provided your thoughts **are clear and** well arranged ; and they ought **to be so** before **you put pen to** paper." In the Preface to the first edition of Shakespeare, the editors say **of** him, " His

mind and hand went together : and what he thought, he
uttered with that easiness that we have scarce received
from him a blot in his papers." Much "copy" was thus
sent by Durivage to the printer without a blot; but often
in prose and always in verse he showed he knew that per-
fection can be approximated only at the expense of un-
sparing erasures and interlineations. Some of his lyrics
which he was supposed to have thrown off carelessly, had
really been subjected by him to the most patient *labor
limæ ;* to this they owe their exquisite finish and their
wide popularity. The very ones in which he himself
recognized the greatest ease and nature were those that
had been the most slowly elaborated. Some of them,
indeed, seemed to be dashed off at a heat, but it was the
white heat of a fire that had long been burning within
him. For surviving relatives and friends another secret
charm of his best verse is that, at least between the lines,
it is deeply, even when unconsciously, autobiographical.
Still another charm which some of the poems in this col-
lection possess is their dramatic spirit and tone. The
same characteristic belonged to the historical romances
and the novelettes and even the character-sketches with
which he so profusely supplied the weekly "story-
papers" and magazines. Each story had a carefully
constructed plot, it abounded in natural and appropriate
dialogue and, throughout, it was full of dramatic action.
His novels and stories have therefore been justly called
"masterpieces of current fictitious literature."

Mr. Durivage was the anonymous author of a number
of acting plays. He wrote one drama, " Monaldi," based

on the exquisite tale, bearing that title, by Washington
Allston, the celebrated American artist and poet, Coleridge's and the elder Dana's friend, to whose genius that
of Durivage was closely akin. Miss Laura Keene, a
competent judge, said of Durivage's "Monaldi," after
weighing every word of it, that "it was the best American
play ever written," and a similarly favorable opinion was
pronounced by one of the ablest critics of New England.
Even in the mutilated form in which it was unfortunately
produced a few years ago at a New York theatre, it had a
successful run, and if restored to the form in which the
author offered it for presentation, it would be sure to retain
a high and permanent rank on the stage. Mr. Durivage
himself made of his original play a French version, which
a Regnier, D'Ennery, or a Sardou would find ready, with
but very slight modifications, to be brought out successfully
in Paris. Mr. Durivage made an excellent translation of
Victor Hugo's "Ernani," and prepared it for the American stage. His own taste led him, as a play-writer, to
the refined, romantic, and sentimental, "but," to cite his
words, "the public now seeks the stage for amusement
solely. Goldsmith wrote 'She Stoops to Conquer,' a five
act farce—but exquisite foolery—which will flout forever,
while many a splendid argosy has gone to the bottom.
Gaudeamus igitur !" So, toward the end of his busy
career, Mr. Durivage, whose comic sketches under the
signature of "The Old 'Un" had placed him in the front
rank of American humorists, and whose life-long study of
the stage and its requirements eminently qualified him to
be a successful comic dramatist, undertook and completed

an American character comedy entitled "Dead Broke." The popular predilection is for plays of this sort, as the success of Solon Shingle, Colonel Sellers, Mose, Bardwell Slote, Rip Van Winkle, and Davy Crockett testifies. The days of deep tragedy and sanguinary melodrama have passed away. People go to the theatre to laugh and not to weep. Besides, comic play-writing has another recommendation which is not to be despised—"there's millions in it."

Mr. Durivage's literary ventures, it has been remarked, all proved successful. He had, to a high degree, the tact of an experienced journalist in choosing the right subjects at the right time. Always keeping punctually his engagements with publishers, he belonged to the first of the two classes into which some philosopher, who had perhaps himself been a publisher, has divided not only the world of authors, but all mankind—the reliable and the unreliable. His knowledge of human nature, and his familiarity with business habits, spared him many annoyances of which authors, and particularly the *genus irritabile* of poets, often complain, with or without reason. His literary and editorial work commanded not only the interest and approval of the public, but also a ready market and liberal pay among publishers. Much of this work, although not of a kind to win for him personal fame, enabled him to acquire a handsome competency, in addition to savings from his salary as a Government official. His case would be in point as an illustration of the benefits which would accrue to the public as well as to a worthy class of citizens capable of deserving well of the nation, both by their honest discharge of administrative duties and their assiduous cultivation of literary studies, if such a thoroughly organized civil service should be put into operation as many far-sighted reformers have proposed and as, at length, a President of the United States has been found intelligent and generous enough to approve. In 1843 Mr. Durivage was appointed Inspector of Customs in his native city, and he most satisfactorily filled similar positions for many years, until 1860, without any abatement, but rather to the advantage of his literary and artistic pursuits. Under President Franklin Pierce's administration (1853–1857) he was appointed at first Private Secretary to Charles H. Peaslee, Collector for the port of Boston, then Clearance Clerk, and, still later, Assistant Deputy Surveyor. In each and all of these positions he became an expert ; and, to the credit of that Boston culture at which too many dunces aim their pointless jests, his quality of man of letters was not allowed to bar his claims to recognition as a first-rate official. In China, where civilization, or at least the civil service, is further advanced than with us, Mr. Durivage might have confidently looked forward to becoming a mandarin of the ninth class, with corresponding emoluments, embroideries, cap, and "little round button on top." Even in England his advancement by regular grades would have been sure and encouraging. The names of Charles Lamb, author of "Elia," Hoole, the translator of Tasso, and James Hill, the historian of British India, are not more honorably and pleasantly identified with the East India House in Leadenhall street, London, in which

2

they were clerks, than are those of Nathaniel Hawthorne
and Francis Durivage with the Boston Custom House.
" My printed works," said Lamb, "were my recreations
—my true works may be found on the shelves in Leadenhall street, filling several hundred folios." Hawthorne
and Durivage might have said something like this.
What delightful reminiscences might have been pre-
served of these two " Custom House Inspectors Extraordinary," by any one who had the good fortune to meet
them strolling together along Boston wharves, or chat-
ting on board picturesque looking craft that from foreign
ports brought to them richer cargoes by far, in the shape
of associations, aids for reflection, hints and " motives "
for song, tale, or essay, than any treasures invoiced to
solid or stolid ship-owners. What a joy and what food
for memory to have shared an interview between these
two impressionable and thoughtful men in the little back-
room at the Old Salt House, where the genial " Jim
Oakes" was fond of welcoming them and other wits and
notabilities of his day. Oakes himself, like most of his
chosen friends, has now passed away. How he must
have been missed by the birds that he used to feed from
his hand early in the morning on Boston common ! If
they had sung his requiem, the burden of their song
would have been :

> " He prayeth well who loveth well
> Both man and bird and beast.
> He prayeth best who loveth best
> All things both great and small ;
> For the dear God who loveth us
> He made and loveth all."

Until his death Mr. Oakes kept up an intimate correspondence with his friend Durivage, after the latter left Boston to live in New York.

If, as Miss Martineau justly contends, the right of freedom of epistolary speech were not too sacred to be violated by making biographical material of the written confidences of friends, a bright and interesting volume might be compiled from the private letters of Durivage. He was an unsurpassed letter-writer, and neither Cicero nor Montaigne better understood and practised than he the divine philosophy of friendship, which somehow seems to be growing obsolete—and the more's the pity—in these days of postal cards and telegrams and general selfishness. Even had he led for thirty years in Paris the life of suicidal isolation which is wretchedly led by far too many members of the American colony here, Durivage could never have become so thickly incrusted with selfishness as to forget any one whom he had once known as a friend. " Friends once, friends for life," was his unchanging motto.

Durivage was not only a model correspondent, but an incomparable travelling companion, as his friends Burnham and Ballou can testify. He had long cherished the idea of "completing his education," as he used to say, by foreign travel. It had cost him no little self-denial to resist the temptations offered him by several skippers and owners, in the way of free passages to distant ports while he was at the Boston Custom House. In fact, like the celebrated essayist, John Forster, and many eminent *savants*, he had studied maps and illustrated books of travel so extensively and minutely, and had so finely

trained his conceptive faculty, that he knew more about
most countries than many who had visited them. In
imagination he had often circumnavigated the globe.
None knew better, or more highly appreciated than he,
the utility and the pleasures of foreign travel, and when,
at length, it became convenient for him to make the
tours abroad which he had planned and dreamed of long
beforehand, his previous knowledge of history and of
several modern languages, as well as of geography, greatly
facilitated his enjoying and profiting by them. But he
came home from these tours abroad all the more patri-
otic an American. All that Europe can teach America
he clearly saw and acknowledged, but it did not blind
him to all that Europe has yet to learn from America.

Even what Jefferson used to call the "damp and
gloomy climate of Paris" could not prevent Durivage
from surrendering himself wholly to that maniacal passion for what he called the "most fascinating city in the
world"—a passion which never releases any one whom it
has once bewitched. That fever is incurable, and it
attacks, more or less, all who have ever seen with their
own eyes the towers of the Cathedral of Notre Dâme de
Paris and the dome of the Pantheon. In truth, it is not
surprising that, like almost every one else who has felt,
as he did, on arriving in Paris, that "his foot was on his
native heath," if his name were not McGregor, or at least
that he ought to have been born here and that he was
bound to live here—he was smitten with admiration for
this wonderful city, and suffered always after leaving it
from that *nostalgie de Paris* which torments all exiles

from it. Few born **Parisians, or** Parisianized provincials
and foreigners, ever knew Paris better **or** loved it more,
in spite of all its faults, than Durivage. It was **only in**
his very last letter to me **that I** detected any sign of his
relaxing his hold on the firm hope which had long
promised that he should yet return here once more, if
only, as he said, "to arrange with the service of the
Pompes Funèbres for his burial in *Père la Chaise* or
Montmartre, or some other Parisian cemetery. But, **on**
the other hand, **none** could more fully enjoy than Durivage, by way of contrast to "the damp and gloomy
climate" of Paris, **the** warmth, purity, splendor, and ex-
hilaration of our **own glorious** climate. **Nor was** ever
any philanthropist more deeply pained than was he by
what Jefferson deplored as "**the needless** misery of man"
in the most favored regions of Europe. Moreover,
Durivage was so dear a lover of home itself that sheer
home-sickness often unexpectedly interrupted his tours
abroad, and he arrived at last to the conclusion that "if
we could but so divide ourselves as to stay at home **at**
the same time, travelling would be one of the greatest
pleasures, and of the most instructive employments in
life."

Among his **chief** pleasures in travelling abroad Durivage counted his visits to galleries of art, **the** society of
artists, both European and American, and the manifold
incitements and satisfactions which, as himself an amateur artist, he derived from scenery and life in Europe.
At home, likewise, his artistic eye was ever open to the
picturesque in scenery and life. Many a picture within

the silent galleries of his mind might well have been trans-
ferred to canvas. When quite young, he had hesitated
whether to devote himself to art or to literature, " the
supreme fine art." He never entirely abandoned **his**
study of art, and he exhibited rare taste and considerable
skill in painting both landscapes and figures. **He greatly**
estimated the potential value of the highest kinds of
portrait painting, **as** exemplified in certain immortal
works by Titian, Velasquez, Gainsborough, or some
other master who **gives not** only the subject as he may
have looked **in common life, but the whole substance of**
his character, the " form **and pressure** " of his mind, **so
far** as these inner features are stamped on **the outward.**
Such are pictures wherein " the artist has divined that
one comprehensive look, the presence of which hardly
the most intimate friends could remember, but which
really seemed **to** render the man's whole individuality."
It may, indeed, be as impossible, in some cases, as
Southey says of the portrait of Dr. Daniel Dove, to paint
the character which constitutes the identity of a countenance, as to paint the flavor of an apple or the fragrance
of the rose. But it is not too much to say that several
of the portraits **from the hand** of Durivage which adorn
the Custom Houses of Boston and New York—as for
instance, the portrait of General **Lincoln, the first Col-**
lector of the Port of Boston, that of David Henshaw,
and those of Collector Henry Smythe, and Charles P.
Clinch, brother **to** Mrs. A. T. Stewart, and, for nearly
forty years Deputy Collector of the Port of New York—
attain, to a remarkable degree, what Palgrave rightly

defines to be "the first, second, and third essentials in portraiture, namely, matterful grasp over human features as the embodiment of human character." Durivage lost no opportunities of showing that he was one of the most intelligent and of the most generous art critics. If he ever seemed to be too lenient, it was because he took into consideration the peculiar difficulties and obstacles with which American artists still have to struggle, and the fact that, in its present stage, American art needs wise encouragement rather than carping criticism. None could criticise more severely when he deemed it his duty so to do. But the higher his own ideal of excellence the more indulgent he was toward those who made earnest, even if inadequate, efforts to reach it. In his miscellaneous writings, as in his art criticisms, it was often happily apparent that, like Hazlitt and Thackeray, he had learned to handle not only the pen but also the pencil.

Durivage had so hearty a contempt for shams of all sorts, and especially for the cant of the professed philanthropist, and he was so strongly devoted to the Union and the Constitution of the United States, that he had but little patience with those dangerous agitators, as he deemed them, who endangered the Union by attacking the Constitution under pretext of seeking the immediate abolition of negro slavery. On this subject his views coincided more nearly with those of Rev. Dr. Garnett, Rev. Dr. Adams, Mr. Choate, and Mr. Webster, and other worthy men whose conscientiousness, humanity, and patriotism the wildest radicals could not deny, even when stigmatizing them as "old fogies behind the times," than with those proclaimed by William Lloyd Garrison and Theodore Parker. In short, he was an old fashioned democrat. But he was a democrat in a higher and wider than a partisan sense. He was a devout worshipper of true liberty. He believed with constancy in the certain increase of popular interest and the ultimate demolition of all injurious power held by the few against the many. He believed in securing the greatest good of the greatest number. He did not share the kind of religious terror under the impression of which De Tocqueville avowed that he wrote his famous book entitled "Democratie en Amérique"—a terror inspired by the sight of "that irresistible revolution which has marched for so many centuries through all obstacles, and is still marching on, in the midst of the ruins it has made." Durivage took a less gloomy view of this irresistible democratic resolution. He saw, as Mr. W. E. Forster, in his address as Lord Rector of the University of Aberdeen, November 4, 1876, remarked, that "there is no mincing the matter, unless the world goes back, democracy must go forward. The will of the people must more and more prevail. We cannot prevent numbers ruling ; we can only persuade them to rule well." Durivage never lost the interest awakened in him by the revolutionary movements in Europe in 1848. Although he regretted and abhorred the atheism and the tyrannical destruction of individual liberty incorporated in Russian Nihilism and French Communism by certain leaders of the revolutionary movement of to-day in Europe, nevertheless he persisted in hoping that in due time the stream of revolution will be purged of all evil obstructions, and will flow quietly on, unstained by blood, and spreading fertility and happiness among the nations. He did not deem it Utopian to expect the establishment, one of these days, of an enlightened, prosperous, and powerful republican confederacy, that should be in fact, if not in name, the United States of Europe, a worthy counterpart of the United States of America. He kept unabated his early enthusiasm for Garibaldi, who was once agreeably surprised at being greeted by Durivage as "Liberator of Rome and Italy," on presenting for examination the papers of the little vessel which he commanded on one of his voyages to South America. After duly certifying the papers, Durivage, bare-headed, escorted the hero and patriot all the way down the long flight of stairs leading from the Boston Custom House, and bade him adieu with more show of reverence than he would have manifested to any hereditary king. The astonished crowd of clerks and sea-captains who witnessed the scene, did not know at first what to make of this deviation from the cool and somewhat formal demeanor of Durivage toward ordinary visitors to the Custom House. But Garibaldi was no ordinary visitor. Another leader of the European democracy, Victor Hugo, was always held in enthusiastic admiration by Durivage. No more sincere or eloquent tribute was received by the venerable poet and orator when he recently entered upon his eightieth year, amidst the applause of Europe and the world, than the verses which Durivage sent to

2*

him. If the transatlantic praise of contemporaries be at once a foretaste and a pledge of the fame to be conferred by posterity, the illustrious old man must have **been** deeply gratified by Durivage's little poem "To Victor Hugo;" and as the writer of it, alas! died before it reached the eye for which it was destined, it chimed in with the multitude of other songs of honor on that rare occasion like a voice *d'outre tombeau* as well *d'outre mer.* **As** for France, "his beloved France," as Durivage was fond of calling her, he never despaired of her. With Sir Erskine **May, the historian of** "Democracy in Europe," he extolled her, after all her trials, as "yet great **and** powerful and high, if not the first in **the** scale **of** civilized nations. Blessed with recuperative powers beyond those of any other state, she is rapidly effacing the scars of war and revolution ; and, profiting by the errors of the past, she may yet found a stable government, enjoying the confidence of all classes and worthy of her greatness and enlightenment."

Mr. Durivage was married on the **14th** of October, 1833, to Miss Almira Aldworth, whose native gentleness and refinement, whose serenity and uniform self-control under all changes of scene and circumstance, whose **un-**failing sympathy, whose

> "Reason firm, and temperate will,
> Endurance, foresight, strength, and skill,"

in fine, **whose** whole stock of high womanly qualities confirmed her husband in his theory that even artists and literary men are not necessarily excluded from the paradise of married life, but may hope, on the contrary and on right conditions, to enjoy its blessings as much, at least, as other men. Sometimes, indeed, it would seem that none need more or appreciate more fully than artists and men of letters, with their peculiar susceptibilities and the incessant draft of their pursuits on their supply of nervous force, the repose and sweet recuperative influences which home alone can give. But the happiest home is not safe against the intrusion of death, and Mr. Durivage had the misfortune of losing his beloved wife on the 6th of December, 1869. His daughter Mary Ritchie, who has now the melancholy pleasure of remembering that all was done that could be done to alleviate her father's sufferings during the last painful days of his life, was early trained by him to hold the pleasant relation of companion and associate, as well as daughter, and even in her girlhood he gladly counted, as he often has told me, on her aid and encouragement in his favorite literary and artistic pursuits. His two sons, fine manly lads, who warranted his proudest hopes of their possible future, joined the Federal army soon after the outbreak of our late Civil War. Both were on General B. F. Butler's staff. The elder son, Francis Alexander, was born April 14, 1836, and died February 11, 1864. The younger, Henry Aldworth, born June 22, 1837, was drowned in the Mississippi, April 23, 1862, while commanding a troop of cavalry of picked men, at the taking of Fort Jackson. After the sudden death of his younger son, Mr. Durivage removed to New York, to be near his only daughter, who had married an enterprising and prosperous merchant of that city. His beloved grandchildren, Harry and Alice Bennett, were to grow up **and** fill in his affection the aching void made by the loss of his wife and sons. In 1862 he accepted in the New York Custom House a responsible position, which he resigned in 1867 ; when he went to Europe in company with Captain George P. Burnham, visiting England, Scotland, Ireland, France, Germany, and Switzerland. After the death of his wife, in 1869, **Mr.** Durivage again crossed the Atlantic, visiting France, Holland, Belgium, and Prussia, and returning to the United **States at the** outbreak of the Franco-Prussian war. **In** 1873–74, in company with his friend, Mr. Ballou, he **visited France and** Italy. **He** again went to Europe in the spring of 1875, but **he returned home within a** few weeks. On his return voyage, about eight days before reaching the port of New York, he was stricken **with** paralysis, which rendered him **partially** helpless, although leaving his mind perfectly bright **and clear until** January 31, 1881, when he had another shock, from which he never rallied, dying after a prostration of only thirty-six hours, **in the** sixty-seventh year of **his** age.

Durivage was gifted by nature with a superb constitution, both bodily and mental. His torso would have been the admiration of a great sculptor. His voice came, rich and strong, from the depths of his chest. For many **years he** enjoyed almost perfect health, being singularly **exempt from the ills to** which a sedentary life dooms almost all whom it enchains. At length **he** paid dearly for this rare **exemption,** although **his** strength in struggling **with** disease seemed almost miraculous. The final agony was brief but terrible, and his vain efforts to speak when stricken for the last time were very distressing. But as during his prolonged illness the lessons of "Life in a Sick-room" (powerfully taught by Miss Martineau, from her own experience, in an excellent little book with that title) had silently sunk into his character, gradually and surely unfolding its noblest traits, so, no sooner had his spirit been released from its earthly prison and taken its flight "along the line of limitless desires," than an almost magical bodily transfiguration followed. All traces of years of pain, weariness, and anxiety disappeared from his countenance. "He seemed to be but thirty years of age;" and the last farewell look of the mourners around him revealed in his face a beauty and peace which they never remembered to have seen there during his life. "I never saw him look so young, handsome, and happy," said Mr. Hanscom, one of his closest friends. The light from above that had shone upon him while he was groping through the valley of the shadow of death now illuminated his very features in a way symbolical of heavenly bliss in the future. While confined to his sick-room, Durivage once wrote, after briefly alluding to some inevitable causes for despondency : "But how much is left for which I hourly give thanks to God. *Me dea super est !* and if I wish to live a little longer it is to testify my gratitude to God by doing some good to some of his creatures." He often expressed his thankfulness for the unfailing sympathy of all his friends, and particularly for the tender and prayerful interest which his cousin in religion, Sister Frances, and other pious Sisters of St.

Joseph's, at Emmetsburg, **Maryland**, manifested in his temporal and spiritual welfare. His heart was **truly** Catholic in its charity, embracing all good and beautiful souls, of whatever religious creed. One of the most faithful and welcome visitors to his sick-room was an "Israelite without guile," a man, like himself, of extraordinary vitality in body and mind, who once journeyed on foot, more than forty years ago, all over Europe, from St. Petersburg to Constantinople, and whose remarkable experiences on both sides of the Atlantic were, **scarcely** less than his rare superiority of character, deeply interesting to Durivage.

I cannot more fitly close this hurried and **imperfect** biographical sketch of my dearest friend than by **tran**scribing the words **of** the survivor of the two brothers who wrote "Guesses at Truth." Referring to the lamented "partner of all his thoughts and feelings," Julius Charles Hare said of his brother: "He too is gone. But is he lost to me? O no! He whose heart was ever pouring forth **a** stream of love, the purity and inexhaustibleness of which betokened its heavenly origin, as he was ever striving to lift me above myself, is still at my side, pointing my gaze upward. Only, the love which was hidden within him, has now overflowed and transfigured **his** whole being; and his earthly form is turned into that of an angel of light."

POEMS.

THE GLENALOON; OR, THE SKIPPER'S YARN.*

ONLY a ripple, and just a puff
  Stirring the old brown sails,
Like as a breath from a sick man's lips
  Flutters a bit, then fails.
After awhile the wind was dead,
  And we rolled on the oily sea,
Like a weary man in a fever fit
  Moving uneasily.

No headway on the old barky now !
  She might have been a log.
Ten leagues away the land lay hid
  By a strip of cold, gray fog :
And three points off the starboard bow—
  'Twas a summer night in June—
Where the sky and the water joined in one,
  Heaved up the red, full moon.

* Founded on fact.

Bloody red, but silver soon,
   With a path of glittering light
Stretched from the bark to the ocean's edge,
   Waving, and broad, and bright.
Something dark in the shining **belt,**
   About a league away,
A shapeless **bulk,** like a **ragged** rock,
   On the face of the water lay.

There was no rock or reef on the chart
   Laid down as here about ;
We looked through the night-glass steadily
   But we couldn't make it out.
I **kept my eye on the ugly thing**
   As I stood on the quarter-deck,
Then ordered the crew to lower the gig—
   It **might** be it was a wreck.

We pulled away for the shapeless hulk
   Till it loomed against the moon,
And we read on the bow of a mastless brig
   The name—the " Glenaloon."

We hailed, tho' never a man was on deck,
   And never a voice replied ;
We shipped our oars as we touched the wreck,
   And climbed the vessel's side.

There was a rubbish of splintered spars—
   Mainmast and foremast gone—
Shattered boats on the littered deck,
   But of living beings—none !
Surely that is a human form
   Crouching upon the deck,
In an old sou' wester and Guernsey frock !
   "Shipmate ! what of the wreck ? "

Surly old chap ! I raised his hat—
   Remember, the moon was full—
And started back, for its white rays fell
   On a ghastly, grinning skull.
Groping our way through spars and sails,
   Mottled with shade and light,
Five more skeletons we found
   Bleached to a deathly white.

Then walking aft—the deck was flush—
  To the cabin I made my way.
Stretched on the transom at full length
  The skeleton captain lay.
In his bony hand a paper was clutched
  (I read what it said next day),
" Wrecked—boats stove and food all gone—
  We can but wait and pray."

      .

As we pulled from the brig o'er the steel-black sea,
  In the light of the pitiless moon,
We read again her fateful name—
  The weird name—" Glenaloon."
And faster and faster into the waves
  The blades of our stout oars fell,
For the deck seemed swarming with shadowy forms
  Waving a wild farewell.

In the sunny calm of the following day
  We buried the fleshless crew.
Shrouded and shotted, one by one,
  They sank through the water's blue

And I never look of a summer night
  On the blood-red disk of the moon,
But I think of the horror she once revealed—
  The wreck of the " Glenaloon."

AUTUMN MUSINGS.

ONLY the dates of birth and **death**,
  In faded ink on a faded leaf,
Call up a spasm of sobbing breath
  And loosen the fountain of bitter grief.

The leaves are bright with a thousand tints
  Dropping from autumn's coronal,
Bright as the visions of vanished youth—
  Bright as my hopes before their fall.

Ah ! then my spirit is very sad,
  And I bow to the tempest sweep of grief,
And, thinking of her I loved and lost,
  I cry, " Oh God ! is there no relief ? "

Then, ere I lay the Book aside,
  With a heart by cruel anguish torn,
I read, in the blaze of sudden light,
  The sentence, " Blessed are they that mourn ! "

And I know the light is the light of truth,
  And the words the words of Him who trod,
With bleeding feet, the paths of earth,
  And, through sorrow, paved the way to God.

And a face smiles out from the parting clouds,
  Bright, with a brighter day than ours ;
Round it no tempest of autumn leaves,
  But the bloom of a myriad deathless flowers.

October, 1870.

FIFINE OF NORMANDY.

A PEASANT maiden of Normandy,
Heart-whole and bright, with footstep free,
With sweet brown eye and clustering curls
Exactly like one of Greuze's girls.
If *la creuse casée* you chance to have seen
You have an idea of Josephine.

Months pass on and the Norman maid
Has gone to Paris to learn a trade.
Whose coupé is that sweeping by the lake
With an Englishman galloping in its wake ?
The blush has gone from the pretty face,
And a layer of rouge has taken its place,
For the woollen scarf there's a fichu of lace,
And she smokes a cigar with insolent grace.
" Egad ! " cries Milor, " she's going the pace ! "

The nets of St. Cloud have drawn a prize
Gazed on by horror-stricken eyes,
Commented on with bated breath :
For even *flâneurs* are awed by death.
So young in years and so passing fair,
To reach the extreme of fell despair !
Mute are the lips that sang with glee,
But a few months back, *Ma Normandie !*
Yet sighs are uttered and tears are shed
Over the form of the unknown dead.

There's a little hillock on Mont Parnasse
With a scanty layer of shrivelled grass ;
On the little cross above it is seen
Nothing but this—*Cigit Fifine.*

TO H. H., A DEAR GERMAN FRIEND.

HERMANN ! I daily bless the hour
   When first I clasped thy trusty hand,
And felt the friendship proffered me
   Immovably would stand.

When, sorrow darkening over me,
   I pressed a weary bed of pain,
Thy sympathetic words and smiles
   Revived my hope again.

Mein bruder! Words can ne'er express
   The gratitude that fills my soul,
That hours do but tensify,
   As, hurrying past, they roll.

I know I share thy inmost thoughts,
   That all our sympathies are joined,
Each heart-beat answers one of thine—
   Leb' wohl, mein lieber Freund !

LOVE AND REASON.

In ages long past, when the Paphian bower
  Was dear to the graces and sacred to love,
With a song like a zephyr's, from flower to flower,
  There soared in its shadows a beautiful dove.
And the heart of young Cupid with rapture was stirred,
By the voice of Ianthe caressing her bird.

But Cupid, for constantly vexing his mother,
  Neglecting the duties assigned to his care,
Committing offences one after another,
  Was banished a season from Paphos the fair.

With Reason to tutor him into his duty,
  His plumage all clipped (for he strove to be free),
They carried him far from the bower of beauty
  To where a lone island arose from the sea.
Love wept, for no longer to soothe him he heard
Ianthe's soft voice or the notes of her bird.

3

One eve as they gazed on the day that was dying
  In the western pavilion of crimson and blue,
A silver-winged dove through the sunset came flying
  And bore from Ianthe a kind billet-doux.
Both snatched at the treasure, but breathed not a word,
While Love got the letter and Reason the bird.

————

SCOTLAND. ¹

Fair Scotland ! many days have passed
  Since first I viewed thy mountains hoary,
And, standing on thy hallowed soil,
  Reviewed thy old historic story.
For not alone art thou renowned,
  For lake and mountain, hill and glen—
All beauties dear to artist eye—
  The mother thou of noblest men.

Pre-eminent in warlike deeds,
  As steel to hilt supremely true,
The laurel chaplet they have borne
  From Bannockburn to Waterloo.

In Belgic land, in Asian sands,
  Beneath old Egypt's brazen sky.
Wrapped in the bonny Tartan plaid,
  The bones of Scotia's children lie.

But to a dearer theme than war,
  The memory reverently turns,
And holds to light the scroll that bears
  The names of Wilson, Scott, and Burns.
The windings of the silver Tweed,
  "The banks and braes of bonnie Doon,"
Seen through the halo of romance,
  Beneath the smiling skies of June.

Old Arthur's Seat, and Holyrood,
  Melrose and Dryburg's ruined fanes,
The mountain gray, the dusky wood,
  Shall I behold thee once again?
But should an evil fate forbid,
  No change or chance can ever blot,
Those pictures from my heart of hearts,
  Dear land of Walter Scott.

IN MEMORY OF WILLIAM S. BARTLETT.

SIT TERRA TIBI LEVIS.

LIGHT rest the earth above the form
  I knew so well of old,
The casket modelled out of clay,
  To hold a heart of gold.

In the old well-remembered years
  I never, never heard,
From the dear lips I loved so well,
  A single unkind word.

But I have often seen him weep
  O'er others' sins and woes ;
Hence, sweet shall be his final sleep
  And placid his repose.

His virtues in surviving hearts
  Shall live, a sacred trust—
The lapse of time can ne'er corrode.
  The treasure of the just.

But to his name a brighter fame
A deathless lustre gives ;
We know that he has passed away,
And, *therefore*, that he lives

With kindred spirits, pure as his,
In realms forever blest,
Where cloudless skies smile down upon
The home of perfect rest.

New York, December 7, 1878.

———

IN MEMORIAM OF ROBERT DUFF.

An Impromptu.

Too late I learned that he had passed away
To place one flower upon his funeral pall,
A single leaf, a blossom, or a spray,
To grace the tributary coronal.

Hence, to the honor of departed worth,
This humble tribute of an honest pen,
To him who, while a denizen of earth,
Ranked with the kindliest and best of men.

He wore no mask ; the radiance of his soul
   Illumed each feature of his honest face.
Kindness and charity, fidelity,
\ Whoever looked upon the man could trace.

To see him was to trust him, and to know
   To love him. Thousands can attest
That those who knew him most loved him best.

Duty and Truth, and Charity and Love
   Were his companions in the path he trod,
An humble path, perhaps, but one that leads
   The pilgrim's footsteps to the throne of God.

Few men were like him, for it is confessed,
   That we have fallen upon an evil day,
When Gold allures and Self is paramount,
   And those most trusted readiest obey.

But they who trusted him whose death we mourn
   Felt their assurance founded on a rock.
Proof to temptation's manifold assaults—
   The bad man's stratagem and the scoffer's mock.

So 'tis a heart of gold, proven and tried,

   Mouldering to dust beneath the verdant sod,

Trite is the saying, but forever true—

   " An honest man's the noblest work of God."

AU REVOIR.

He stood in the stirrups, one hand on the rein ;

The enemy's bugles rang shrill from the plain.

A lady of rank, with a look full of pain,

Placed a spotless white rose in the gauntletted hand,

That was far more familiar with pistol and brand.

She whispered "Adieu !" but he said, " *Au revoir !*

I carry a charm to the vortex of war ;

This token shall safety and victory gain—

You soon shall see me and your white rose again."

A thunder of hoofs, and a thunder of steel,

Like an eagle the squadrons of Magyars wheel,

And back from their charge the fierce Muscovites

   reel.

But out of the earthquake and carnage of war

One blood-sprinkled charger brings backs a hussar.

He rode on the spur to the countess's door,
And still his right hand the sweet love-token bore.
" Dear Hungary's banner floats high on the plain,
The ruthless invaders are routed or slain ;
By victory laurelled, I greet you again."
But oh ! from his cold lips his color had fled,
And the rose he gave back to her hand was now red.
The battle was won, but her hero was dead.

MY LITTLE SISTERS.

GAZING intent in memory's magic glass,
I see two smiling childish figures pass.
Lucy and Annie ! images most dear,
Tho' lost to earthly sight for many a year.
Brief in this life was their allotted space
To glad our hearts with purity and grace.
God gave and took them—to his angel host
Added the treasures that we prized the most.
Sinless and white, each blessed little heart
Hears the Divine permission to depart.
As I remember them, to me 'tis given
To picture their unshadowed bliss in Heaven.
Their eyes undimmed by even childish tears,

Perpetual flowers around their footsteps spring,

Where birds of paradise are on the wing,

And in the never-ending summer days

Music is one incessant hymn of praise.

The vision passes to recur again,

With power to banish earthly care and pain.

Lucy and Annie! We shall meet again.

OH! NO, HE NEVER MENTIONS IT!

Oh! no, he never mentions it—

   To hope would be absurd—

The last of that five-dollar bill

   I certainly have heard.

I dun him, but a joke he makes

   Of what is my regret;

And when he wins a smile from me

   He thinks that I forget.

They tell me he is happy now—

   They say it is "his way;"

And wish that I may get it when

   I sometimes think he'll pay.

3*

He's gay as any butterfly,
  Forgetful of his debt,
But if he stood within my shoes
  He never could forget.

They bid me go and seek for change
  (What bitter mockery !)
If I by thieves were overhauled
  They'd find no " change " on me.
'Tis true that he frequents no more
  The "alley " where we met,
When " ten strikes " he was wont to score,
  But how can I forget ?

———

THE IRISH VOLUNTEERS.

THE drum and trumpet call to arms,
  The banner waves on high,
And with its stripes and starry folds
  In beauty fills the eye.

Old Massachusetts hears the call,
   And answers it with cheers ;
But who among the first responds?
   'Tis the Irish Volunteers !
      Then hip ! hip ! hip !
      Hurrah ! hurrah !
      For the Irish Volunteers.

The lovely isle that gave them birth
   They love, as men should do ;
But to the land that welcomed them
   Brave sons they'll prove and true.
Against the levelled bayonet,
   Where death his form uprears,
Who'll farther press or firmer charge
   Than the Irish Volunteers ?
      Then hip ! hip ! hip !
      Hurrah ! hurrah !
      For the Irish Volunteers.

The spirit that in olden time
   The hostile Saxon quelled,
And later, in the old " Brigade,"
   The foes of France repelled,

Shall shine beneath the stripes and stars
  Whene'er the foe appears,
And win new glory for the name
  Of the Irish Volunteers.
          Then hip ! hip ! hip !
          Hurrah ! hurrah !
          For the Irish Volunteers.

When pours the foe his deadly fire,
  And forms his lengthened line,
Then brighter for the battle-cloud
  The Shamrock green shall shine.
When pours the cannon through the ranks
  And gleams the horsemen's spears,
Then Faugh-a-Ballagh ! clear the track
  For the Irish Volunteers.
          Then hip ! hip ! hip !
          Hurrah ! hurrah !
          For the Irish Volunteers.

ONLY A WORD.

Silent so long ! It is not well ;
You said I should hear from you, Mirabelle.
If you only knew what it is to wait,
Lonely and sick and desolate !
I ventured only a word to ask
From the friend who spares you the writer's task.
A ring at the door ! The letter has come,
Like a fluttering dove that has found its home.
I rend the envelope with feverish haste,
By the hand of a friend the address is traced.
But the light leaf falls from my hand like lead,
I asked for one word : they have sent it—*Dead !*

THE LION'S BRIDE.

From the German of Chamisso.*

With myrtle-leaves crowned, for her bridal arrayed,
The keeper's fair daughter, a rosy-cheeked maid,
Trips into the den of the lion, who lies
At his mistress's feet, with delight in his eyes.

* This poem inspired Gabriel Max to produce one of his finest illustrative pictures.

The king of the forest, once tameless and wild,
But tractable grown as an innocent child,
Now bends to the beauty who stands at his side,
Her fair hand caressing his rough tawny hide.

She says, " In the days of our childhood, gone by,
What romps have we had, my old friend, thou and I !
Yet would'st thou in frolics, shake out thy great mane,—
Those merry old play-days will not come again ;
For time brings us changes, and care follows play ;
No child, but a woman, I seek thee to-day.

"Oh, were I a child once again and heart free,
I'd willingly stay, dear old fellow, with thee :
But now I must bow to a husband's command,
And follow his steps to a far distant land.

" He saw me, he liked me, and fancied me fair ;
I accepted his hand—see the wreath in my hair !
But I bid thee good-bye in the sorest distress,
Bear witness these tear-drops I cannot suppress.

" Dost thou quite understand me ?   Be quiet, I pray ;
Don't wear such a frown, and don't shake in that way.
See, my bridegroom is coming to fetch me :   take this
Last token of friendship, dear fellow—a kiss."

The tender lips touched him in kindness, and then
In mighty convulsions he shook the strong den.
The bride in alarm sought to quiet his wrath,
But her power was gone, and he stood in her path.
Defiant and angry, resistless and bold,
The fetterless king of the forests of old.

Without there are cries of distress and alarm,
The bridegroom in agony shouts, "Bring an arm !
My hand will not fail me—the monster shall die !"
And wrath and resolve may be read in his eye.
His poor trembling bride seeks the iron-bound door,
Too late !   A fierce leap brings her down to the floor,
A mass of white garments bedabbled with gore.

And when the dear blood of the maiden was shed
Then low drooped the lion's imperial head ;
Grief-stricken, he laid himself down by the bride,
The musket shot sped to his heart and he died.

SONG.

Written for the 219th Anniversary of the Ancient and Honorable Artillery Company, Boston, June 1, 1857.

I.

Again as the year in its hurrying flight
  Restores us the glory of verdure and flowers,
Do we come as of yore to our festival bright,
  With the garlands of joy to entwine the swift hours.
    From our fathers of old
    Came the trust that we hold,
    That links us together in fetters of gold ;

Chorus.

The pledge we renew to the colors they bore
And will stand to our arms like the heroes of yore.

II.

In the sunshine of peace o'er the sea and the land
  Our star-bedecked banner is gallantly streaming ;
In voiceless repose our dark batteries stand,
  No stain dims the sheen of our bayonets' gleaming.

But the war-trumpets breath
Would call from its sheath
Each sword, and give tongue to each engine of death.

Chorus.

And the nations aroused, like the heroes of yore,
Would march to the field with the colors they bore.

THE SWORD OF JACKSON.

It saw not the light in a conqueror's hand,
  It waved o'er no realm by invasion made gory,
But, drawn by the hero to guard his loved land,
  The sword shall illumine the page of his story.
        Its lightning was given
        By bountiful Heaven
To ward off the bolt that our flag would have riven ;
And bless'd be the sword of the hero so brave
Who bared it in battle our banner to save.

Let no speck of rust its fair surface corrode,
  Let it blaze as when foes shrank in terror before it ;
As when on the armorer's anvil it glowed ;
  Be it bright as the soul of the hero who bore it,

When the cannon's dread peal
And the crashing of steel
Made hirelings the fury of freemen to feel ;
And bless'd be the sword of the hero so brave
Who drew it in battle our banner to save.

When peace was restored to the country he loved,
The warrior returned to the citizen's station,
Till freemen their love and their gratitude proved,
And called him to rule o'er a prosperous nation.
With green laurels wreathed,
And peacefully sheathed,
Slept the blade that sprang forth when the war-trumpet
breathed ;
And bless'd was the sword of the hero so brave
Who bared it in battle his country to save.

No more will our summons awaken the sage
Within his loved hermitage calmly reposing,
Where peace and religion their mild lustrous rays
Bestowed on life's evening and hallowed its closing.
He was summoned away
To the regions of day
Where the just bathe in brightness forever and aye,
And the sword that was drawn his country to save,
Shall guard the repose of the faithful and brave.

THE VOICE OF THE SEA.

It whispers like lovers who whisper of bliss
When wave meets with wave in a passionate kiss ;
It hisses with sibilant, energy, like
The poisonous reptile preparing to strike ;
It thunders like storm-clouds that clash o'er the scene
With fierce electricity streaming between ;
It bellows like cannons whose death-fires glow
When war sounds the trumpet of murder and woe ;
It chants a wild requiem in coraline caves
Where mariners toss in their weltering graves ;
It murmurs as soft as the tones of a flute,
When nightingale, vanquished, sits pensive and mute ;
But its soft moonlight music is changed to a roar,
When the billows charge home on the wild rocky shore.
So changeful the music, in fury or glee,
Of the gentle and beautiful—terrible sea.

ANTOINETTE.

WARMLY sheltered from wind and rain
In a kiosque, Place de la Madeleine,
Some year ago in Paris I met
The little flower-girl Antoinette,
With her soft gray eyes and her braids of jet,
Crowning her head like a coronet,
Avenante, gentille, **mais** *pas coquette.*
When dandies ogled she turned away
And had no smile for *les petits crevés.*
She sat all day in a bower of bloom,
Like a shrine pervaded by sweet perfume,
Incense from roses and mignonette,
And saint-like seemed innocent Antoinette.
Deftly her slender fingers wove
Tokens of friendship and tokens of love,
Tokens for others, *her* heart was free,
And she sang at her task—how joyously !

A Sister of Charity passed one day,
And paused to admire her floral display.
" What joy," said the Sister, " if I could bring
To my patients a floral offering !

But I must not think of it—woe is me !
I'm a very poor Sister of Charity
And have no coin for the florist's fee."
Antoinette's smile was joyous and gay,
" *Comme ça se trouve !* " she hastened to say,
" I am overstocked with flowers to-day,
I cannot sell—I must give them away.
Here's heliotrope and here's mignonette,
And here are roses with dew-drops wet,
A gem like a tear in each calyx set."
" Thanks," said the Sister, " now take from me
This little cross and this rosary—
The gift of a friend ere she sank to rest ;
By our Holy Father the beads were blest,
When you tell them o'er, give a thought to me
And a prayer for poor Sister Rosalie."

It were long to tell how the enemy came
And circled the city with steel and flame ;
How his batteries vomited shot and shell,
How Paris struggled and starved and fell,
How fiends arose to the work of hell !
And flowers there were none to buy or sell.

In the Place Vendôme ! whom have we here
In the jaunty dress of a vivandière ?
With a carbine swinging *en bandoulière*,
With a scarlet cap on her black curls set ?
'Tis our little flower-girl, Antoinette.

Weeks roll on and the terror is past ;
The Versailles troops have entered at last,
Through the Arch of Triumph they storm their way,
But the rebels savagely stand at bay.
Fierce and erect on a barricade,
With the fatal scarlet banner displayed,
Grasping the staff, with her white teeth set,
So the chief has ordered, stands Antoinette.
" *Vive la Commune !* " burst from her lips,
And day grows night in a swift eclipse,
The air is swept by a storm of lead ;
And the little vivandière falls dead.
Through his thick moustache the lieutenant hissed,
As he glanced on the fallen Communiste,
"Take this dead she-devil away and pitch
Her carcass into the nearest ditch !"
But a Sister of Charity, robed in black,
With a thin white hand waved the soldiers back.

" Dare not to touch her ! " she said ; " she's mine,
Ecce signum ! behold the sign ! "
And, pressing a kiss on the gray lips cold,
She lifted the beads and the cross of gold.
" In the maddening whirl of an evil day
Her reason tottered and went astray.]
Swept into the vortex of civil strife,
She sealed her faith with her glad young life ;
And over her body shall prayers be said,
In spite of the cause for which she bled."

THIERS.

A NATION bends in grief to-day,
  And turns its reverential gaze
From all the gauds of earth away
  To one lone grave in Père la Chaise.

Low in the lap of mother earth
  Full many a proud and laurelled head,
Renowned for genius or for worth,
  Lies in that city of the dead.

But when their fame has **passed away**,
  In the long lapse of gathered years,
The world's applause will eternize
  The name of Adolph Thiers.

Faithful among the faithless found,
  He, in his country's darkest hour,
U**praised her, bleeding, from the ground,**
  And gave her back her power.

Aye, 'twas his fortune and his **deed**
  Her pristine greatness **to restore,**
From faults redeemed, from **fetters freed,**
  Far nobler than before.

The baffled foe, in mute amaze,
  Beheld the miracles he wrought,
The bloodless victories of mind,
  Greater than battles fought.

Soon will the day arrive when France
  Can all his services repay.
She needs but **follow** where the dead
  Has marshalled her the way.

No mausoleum consecrate,
  With costly marbles deftly blent,
But the Republic, consummate,
  Be this his monument.

———

THE OLD YEAR AND THE NEW.

A COFFIN passes down the stair,
  A bride taps at the gate ;
A long farewell to Seventy-seven !
  Welcome to Seventy-eight !

Strew flowers upon the bridal path !
  Strew flowers upon the bier !
Tears, salt tears for the dead and gone !
  Smiles for the coming year !

For joy and sorrow ever blend—
  The greeting and farewell,
The tears of grief, the smiles of love,
  The joy-peal and the knell.
    4

So chant the solemn requiem,
  And sing the bridal song ;
Tears to the Old year now are due,
  Smiles to the New belong.

Who comes like Maia, ever sweet,
  With hopes as bright and fair
As flowers beneath the fairies' feet,
  Or song-birds in the air.

Smiles to the bridal feast be given !
  Tears to the funeral state !
A sad farewell to Seventy-seven !
  A cheer to Seventy-eight !

PARIS.

I oft revisit thee in dreams,
  Fair siren of the Seine !
As memory's photographic glass
  Restores thy traits again.

Paris.

I see thee as, when day expires,
   In euthanasia calm,
Glows in the sunset's crimson fires
   The rose of Notre Dame.

And later on, when mists arise,
   And gathering vapors gloom,
Gleams through the dusk the golden dome
   Above Napoleon's tomb.

And is this night? this ardent blaze,
   This universal glow?
A million stars in heaven above,
   Stars in the streets below?

'Tis night, indeed, but this is France—
   No time for slumber here,
Where music summons to the dance,
   And laughter fills the ear.

The reckless reveller repeats,
   As the dizzy hours go by,
" Hurrah ! eat, quaff and laugh to-night,
   To-morrow ye shall die.

" Why call up phantoms of affright,
   And images of sorrow ?
On with the dance ! Mabille to-night !
   Perhaps the Morgue to-morrow ! "

THE LITTLE WHITE MICE.

A Versified Fact.

'Twas night in the silent city,
   The sidewalk covered with ice,
As a little Italian boy chanted,
   " Signori ! my pretty fite mice ! "

In a box from a string depending
   His pets and bread-winners lay,
On crumbs from his scant store feeding,
   Warm nestled in wool and hay.

Up staggered a well-dressed rowdy,
   Excited by drink and play,
One kick sent the little box spinning,
   And the white micè scampered away.

The Little White Mice.

'Twas a stroke of exquisite humor,
  A jest with a flavor of art,
Thus to see the little Italian
  Go off with a broken heart.

The boy sat down on a door-step,
  And his tears fell fast like the rain.
O God! are there none in the city
  To pity and soothe such pain?

A girl sat down beside him,
  As she passed on her weary way;
She placed some coins in his grimy palm
  And wiped his tears away.

For she thought of the little brother
  With whom she used to play,
Ere the spoiler came to the homestead
  On a black and weary day.

" O beautiful, bountiful lady!"
  The little Italian said,
" May our lady her choicest blessings
  Upon and around you shed."
But the young girl said with a shudder,
  " I wish that I were dead!

" Nor penance nor prayer avail me,
  And blessings come all too late,
 On me forever, forever
    Fast locked is the golden gate."

 Nay—for thou still hast charity,
   In spite of the soil of sin,
 And the gate may turn at that blessed word
   And welcome the wanderer in.

JERRY.

His joyous neigh, like the clarion's strain,
When we set before him his hay and grain,
        And the rhythmic beat
      Of his flying feet,
We never, never, shall hear again.
        For the good horse sleeps
        Where the tall grass weeps,
On the velvet edge of the grassy plain,
By the restless waves of the billowy grain,
And never will answer to voice or rein.
By whip-cord and steel he was never stirred,
For he only needed a whispered word
And a tightened rein to fly like a bird.

By loving hands his neck was caressed,
Hands, like his own fleet limbs, at rest.
Through blinding snow, in the murkiest night,
With never a lamp in heaven alight,
With the angry river a sheet of foam,
Swiftly and safely he bore me home ;
And I never resigned myself to sleep
Till I had rubbed him down and bedded him deep.
If I ever can sit in the saddle again,
With foot in stirrup and hand on rein,
I shall look for the like of Jerry in vain.
Steed of the desert or jennet of Spain
Would ne'er for a moment make me forget
My favorite horse, my children's pet,
With his soft brown eyes and coat of jet.

He would have answered the trumpet's peal
And charged on cannon and splintering steel,
But humbler tasks did his worth reveal.
To mill and to market, early and late ;
On the brown field tracing furrows straight,
Drawing the carriage with steady gait—
Whatever the duty we had to ask
Willingly he performed the task.

When his life-work was all complete
He was found in the stable, dead on his feet.
And in spite of each and every fool
Whose brain and heart are hardened by rule,
I have reached the conclusion, that, on the whole,
The horse we loved possessed *a soul !*

A VISION OF THE NIGHT.

I DREAMED I was tossed on a heavy sea
 That rolled to the black horizon's rim,
The stars were drowned in the murky clouds,
 And the lights of Havre were far and dim.

No boat could live in the raging storm
 That broke from a black December sky,
No heart in the icy waves keep warm ;
 Nothing was left me but to die.

Sudden a light around me shone,
 As on dry land a figure stood,
And I raised my wondering eyes, to own
 The loveliest type of womanhood.

Fair and grand was the holy form
 As any Murillo's pencil traced ;
One white hand held a crucifix,
 While spotless lilies the other graced.

And a voice of sweetest music said :
 " Nothing fear—do but follow me ;
Have but faith, and the rock-ribbed earth
 Is less secure than the surging sea."

Soon on the shelving shore I stood,
 Behind the sea with its yawning graves,
And high above, on a steadfast cliff,
 The church of Our Lady of the Waves.*

CHARENTON.

THE window grated! the wicket barred l
Ah! monsieur, they are cruel and hard.
They know I am dying to get away,
For, *voyez vous*, 'tis my wedding-day.

    * At Havre, France, 1873.

4*

I saw her, methinks it was yesterday ;
On her bed in her bridal dress she lay,
White, oh, white as the Jura's snow
Ere the sun has kindled its heart to a glow.

You see, monsieur, I had got my congé
In my little tin box and I hastened away
As only an infantry man can stride
When he hastens to meet his affianced bride.

Through the valley and over the hill,
Past the poplars and past the mill,
Through the orchard and through the gate,
Blithe as a bird that is seeking its mate.

There was the cot with its heavy thatch,
There was the door with its loosened latch.
Softly I raised it—crept up the stair,
And entered the chamber—my love was there.

All alone in the darkened room,
With never a sunbeam to chase its gloom,
But it could not shadow the lovely face,
For that would liven the darkest place.

Playful she ever was, and now,
Tho' I pressed my lips to her fair young brow,
And kissed her hair and her lips—'twas vain,
Never she kissed me back again.

"Sweetheart! You'll kiss me by and by,
Will you not, dearest?" Still no reply.
"Open, I pray thee, those fairest eyes.
The priest is waiting, my love, arise!"

But while I chided her forced delay
The strangest dream stole my wits away.
I dreamed that a Sister of Charity
Rose by the bed from her bended knee.

"Speak not of marriage here," she sighed,
And gently, so gently, led me aside.
"Never will those gray-lidded eyes
Open on yours in glad surprise;

Ne'er on your cheek will you feel her breath—
For she you sought is the Bride of Death.
Bitter tears we all have shed
As we robed the maid for her narrow bed.
She is now at rest. But oh! to you
Tears far bitterer still are due."

That was a tale for a bridegroom gay !
'Twas enough to steal his senses away,
To make a man shriek and tear
In a frenzied fashion his flesh and hair.

It was quite too horrid a dream to last,
Away to the fiends the vision I cast !
But, strange to say, when my mind was clear
I woke to find they lodged me *here*.

Speak, then, kindly, and gently urge,
For they are masters of bond and scourge,
Darkened dungeon and falling shower—
Oh, how well do they know their power !

Yet will they hear if you plead with skill,
They only can sever my bonds at will.
Oh, let me haste to Fanchette, for she
In her bridal raiment is waiting for me.

TO VICTOR HUGO.

MAJESTIC minstrel! Many a year has flown
Since first I heard thy lyre's enchanting tone,
What time, far off in my beloved France,
Thy white plume led the legions of Romance,
Till o'er the ocean, wafted clear and high,
"Victor and Victory!" came the thrilling cry.
And years have flown since, on an evening calm,
I first beheld the towers of Notre Dame.
O'er all the scene thy magic spell was cast;
The Present vanished—I beheld the Past.
The Cour de Miracles disgorged its throng,
Beggars and bravos trooped confused along;
The radiant Archer entered on the scene,
And Esmeralda smote her tambourine.
Then from on high metallic thunder fell
As Quasimodo heaved the ponderous bell.
Since I have noted, through the gathering years,
Thy high career, its triumph and its tears;
Marked thee in exile, seen thy fearless hand,
On crime's low brow affix the burning brand.

Now art thou victor ! Every tempest passed,
Rises serene the steadfast cliff at last.
If on his summit rests a wreath of snow,
'Tis but to hold the sunset's crimson glow,
And o'er the world reflected radiance throw.

BURNING THE LETTERS.

Fragile records of the past,
    Memories frail of joy and woe,
As ye to the flames are cast,
    I will scan ye as ye go.
Winnowing the hoarded pile ;
    All are not to perish here ;
Mixed with words of fraud and guile
    Lines of golden truth appear.

Here is plighted friendship's scroll,
    " Ever faithful " on the seal ;
Time, that provest the honest soul,
    Treason dark did'st thou reveal.
Gracefully the letters flow,
    Yet 'twas but the serpent's trail—
Perish in the fiery glow !
    Be as ashes on the gale !

Black as was the writer's heart
　　Turns his letter in the grate ;
But 'tis gone, and thus depart
　　Both the record and the hate.
Here is flattery's polished phrase—
　　Vanity's emblazoned line—
Feed ye both the fanning blaze,
　　For another instant shine.

Other scrawls to feed the flame !
　　Bridges to a clouded past—
Memories sad of grief and shame —
　　Perish all and perish fast !
" Please destroy," four pages end,
　　Showing how a knave can creep,
Crawl, deceive, and cringe and bend,
　　This I bide my time and keep.

From the camp ! the hand that traced
　　Those few friendly lines are dust ;
Ne'er were war's wild legions graced
　　By leader worthier of trust.

When the field was almost won,
　　Proudly, bravely did'st thou fall—
Thy farewell the pealing gun
　　And the flag thy funeral pall.

Rest thee safe with treasures dear,
　　Words of fond maternal love ;
I've no store of gold—but here
　　Gems I cherish far above
Glittering dross ;—here shine serene
　　Thoughts the coinage of the soul ;
Still to me as it hath been,
　　Light no tempest could control.

Friendship, love, and truth ! ye shine
　　Brighter as the records pale,
And the eyes that scan each line
　　Through forced tears of pleasure fail.
And e'en should time obliterate
　　Every letter of the chart,
These would still escape his hate,
　　They are written on my heart.

HYMN.

GIVER of good ! We lowly bend
  In humble reverence at thy shrine ;
To thee our grateful thanks ascend,
  All that we are and have is thine.

Thine are the fruits and golden grain
  That glow on each autumnal hill,
For thou hast willed the summer rain
  And loosed the fertilizing rill.

Thine are the works this day combined
  To feast the eye and glad the heart,
For thou hast given the strength of mind
  That crown with triumph every art.

Aid us in all that we essay,
  Our aspirations and our might,
Our guide through each laborious day,
  Our sentinel through every night.

REMEMBER THE ALAMO.

WHEN, on the wide-spread battle plain,
The horseman's hand can scarce restrain
His tempered steed that spurns the rein,
    Remember the Alamo, boys,
    Remember the Alamo!

When sounds the thrilling bugle blast,
And "Charge!" from rank to rank is passed,
Then, as your sabre-strokes fall fast,
    Remember the Alamo, boys,
    Remember the Alamo!

Heed not the Spanish battle-yell;
Let every stroke ye give them *tell*,
And let them fall as Crockett fell,
    Remember the Alamo, boys,
    Remember the Alamo!

Remember the Alamo.

For every wound and every thrust,
On pris'ners dealt by hands accurst,
A Mexican shall bite the dust,
Remember the Alamo, boys,
Remember the Alamo!

A cannon's peal shall ring the knell,
Each volley sound a passing bell,
Each cheer Columbia's vengeance tell.
Remember the Alamo, boys,
Remember the Alamo!

For if, disdaining flight, they stand,
And try the issue hand to hand—
Woe to each Mexican brigand!
Remember the Alamo, boys,
Remember the Alamo!

Then boot and saddle! draw the sword;
Unfurl the banner bright and broad,
And as ye smite the murderous horde,
Remember the Alamo, boys,
Remember the Alamo!

MOONLIGHT ON THE HIGHLANDS.

How fair beneath the summer moon
  The varied landscape meets the eye,
And tree and rock, and tower and stream
  Calm in broad effulgence lie !

The stars are smiling from the sky,
  Our sister stars upon the deep,
Where, swinging in the surgeless tide,
  The mariners their vigils keep.

And on the distant headlands dim
  The beacons pour their steady ray,
Lone watchers till the morning beams,
  The sentinels that guard the bay.

The cricket's chirp alone is heard
  To break the stillness of the night,
That wraps in sweet security
  All that is beautiful and bright.

The tree tops, touched with silver, shine,

Wet with the lately fallen shower,

While dark beneath, their **leaves entwine**

In many a dark and tangled bower.

TO ALICE.

WRITTEN IN MY LITTLE GRAND-DAUGHTER'S ALBUM.

How much I love my Alice

No words of mine can tell

Enough my little darling

Knows that I love her well.

I've loved my little Alice

Since first her baby face

Smiled on me like a blossom

Through its pretty veil of lace.

And her brother, bending o'er her,

Stooped down and gently kissed her,

And said with triumph in his **voice,**

" I've got a little sister ! "

May blessings be upon you both,

Love bind you to each other,

And shadows never fall between

The sister and the brother.

April 5, 1878.

THE FLAG ON SUMTER.

DISPLAY once more our standard sheet,
　　Be its broad field " advanced on high,"
And let its constellation meet
　　The brightest sunbeam of the sky.

More sacred far than when it sank
　　From Sumter's staff four years ago ;
The priceless blood has dyed its woof
　　And lent its stripes a ruddier glow.

It floats again to fall no more,
　　But wave in triumph on forever ;
The sun of heaven may set in clouds,
　　But freedom's starry banner—never !

We swear it by the dear remains
　　Of those who fought our land to save,
The blood that dews our battle-plains
　　And hallows every soldier's grave.

Millions of swords shall guard its fame,

In hands of men who never falter ;

The silver stars, the streams of flame

Shall ever deck our country's altar.

THE SLEEP OF NAPOLEON.

The best portrait of the emperor is that which David painted a few hours before his patron's departure for his final campaign. " When now past midnight, instead of retiring to rest, the emperor sent for David, to whom he had promised to sit, and who was waiting in an apartment of the Tuileries. ' My friend,' said Napoleon to the artist, ' there are yet some hours to four, when we are finally to review the defences of the capital; in the meantime, *faites votre possible* (do your utmost) while I read these dispatches,' but exhausted nature could hold out no longer ; the paper dropped from the nerveless hand, and Napoleon sank to sleep. In this attitude the painter has represented him."

I.

CAN'ST thou slumber while on high

Hangs the gathered thunder-cloud,

Hiding all thy native sky

With its black appalling shroud ?

Hearest thou not the sound of fear,

Whispering low of tempest near,

Mighty strife and ruin drear,

Through thine empire proud ?

II.

Thou hast smiled when tempests lowered,
　　And thou sleepest calmly now,
While full many a heart hath cowered,
　　Paling many a lofty brow.
Through thy **heart, to** danger **steeled,**
Through thy hand, that well can **wield**
Battle-blade on stricken field,
　　Calm life's currents flow.

III.

Calm as when at Austerlitz
　　O'er the war-clouds shone **thy star,**
Now obscured and bright **by fits,**
　　Meteor of the stormy **war,**
While thy haughty eagles flew
Lurid smoke of cannon through,
And no glimpse **of** heavenly blue
　　Glimmered from afar.

IV.

Slumber, man of Destiny !
　　Thousands watch o'er thy repose—
Gallant thousands vowed to thee,
　　When thy banner rose.

On their hopes and thine shall fall,
Soon, too soon, a funeral pall.
Rallied by the trumpet call,
  Gather all thy foes.

v.

Like the ravens darkly winging
  To their banquets and their prey,
Sullen soaring, hoarsely singing,
  When the lions stand at bay.
Can'st thou sleep serene and calm,
While the drum in rude alarm,
Summons all thy foes to arm
  For the fatal fray ?

VI.

Scarce can'st thou thy foemen number—
  Yet no dream of death and pain
Pour upon thy peaceful slumber
  Visions of the tented plain.
All thy mighty heart is still—
Yet that heart can rouse at will,
When Destruction's trumpet shrill
  Rings above the slain.

5

VII.

Hero ! warrior ! scourge of God !
　　Sleep, while yet the space is given,
'Ere the green and fragrant sod
　　By the cannon's wheel is riven ;
'Ere thy rowels urge the speed
Of thy fierce and frantic steed
O'er the plain where thousands bleed
　　'Neath the lurid heaven.

VIII.

Sleep ! 'tis well thou can'st not know
　　All the horror of thy fate,
All the wretchedness and woe
　　That upon thy future wait.
He who sits thy throne above,
In His mercy and His love,
Hides the knowledge that would prove
　　Madness to the great.

IX.

Sleep ! and dream of laurels won
　　On old Europe's battle-field,
Of a race in glory run,
　　Of a lofty truth revealed.

Thousands of the proud and free,
Slaves and bondmen but for thee,
In the trying hour will be
    Thy defence and shield.

X.

If thou didst to empire stride
    Over plains bedewed in blood,
Wooing glory as a bride,
    That must sword in hand be woo'd,
Thou dids't only seek to stand
Foremost of a noble band,
Liberator of a land
    Once in servitude.

XI.

Sleep—and wake renewed in might.
    Once again thy blade shall shine,
Through the horrors of the fight,
    All along the blazing line.
Though thou liest with the slain,
Though thou drag'st a captive's chain,
Thou wilt not have lived in vain,
    Glory will be thine !

1838.

THE OLD HOMESTEAD.

Nessun maggior dolore,
Che ricordarsi del tempo felice,
Nell miseria.

—DANTE.

EVER when spring returns
   In the footsteps of winter chill,
When the snow from the woodland path retires,
   The ice from the joyous rill ;
My thoughts go back to the dear old home
   That stands on the breezy hill.

Unchanged to other eyes
   That home of my heart may be,
With its verdant banks and orchard fair,
   But oh, the change to me !

For the voices, save one, are mute
   That filled it in days of yore,
And the sound of feet that I loved to hear
   Is heard in its halls no more—
Afar from the ken of mortal ear
   They are treading the voiceless shore.

The forms of the loved and the lost
  I never shall see again
Rise in the watches of the night,
  Visions of grief and pain.

My mother's stately form
  Bends o'er her favorite flowers,
And I love to think her wandering
  In amaranthine bowers.

The gate is opened wide,
  As it stood on that winter day
When he, our loved and beautiful,
  On his war-horse rode away.

Far, far adown the road,
  His dog ran by his side,
And then crawled back with drooping crest,
  Shivered, and whined and died.

Such omens smite the heart,
  With a keen and sudden pain ;
And we felt that our joy and pride
  Would never return again.

Hence I never more shall climb
    The well-remembered hill,
Though the house still crowns its verdant crest
    And its flowers are springing still.

For the loved of other days
    Are beyond the ice-cold river,
And the voices that poured their joyous lays,
    Are silent, alas ! forever.

SANTA ANNA TO HIS ARMY AT CERRO GORDO.

" MEXICANS ! hear the drum !
    Lo ! the wretched Yankees come !
    Now's the time to give them *some*—
        Arm ye for the fight !

" For your homes and senoritas,
    For your beans and apple-fritters,
    Give the foe a dose of bitters,
        Smite them right and left !

"I'll remain, the army's hope,
  In the rear, and see you cope
  With them through my telescope,
      So be firm and steady.

"So be steady, firm, and brave,
  If you fail the day to save
  I'll entomb me in the grave—
      One foot's already there."

Thus he spoke—on rushed his men
Like lions from a mountain glen ;
But they were sadly whipped again—
      The bloody work was done.

But when red battle's eye was shut
Off on a mule their general put,
And when he should have run and cut
      He only cut and ran.

CHEZ BRÉBANT.

THE vicomte is wearing a brow of gloom
As he mounts the stairs to his favorite room.
"Breakfast for two!" The *garçons* say,
"Then the pretty young lady is coming to-day?"
But the *patron* mutters, "*À Dieu ne plaise!*
I want no clients from Père la Chaise."
Silver and crystal! a splendid show!
And a damask cloth white as driven snow.
The vicomte sits down with a ghastly air—
His *vis-a-vis* is an empty chair.
But he calls to the *garçon*, "Antoine! *Vite!*
Place a chair for the lady's feet!"
"The lady, monsieur?" (in a quavering tone).
"Yes; when have you known me to breakfast alone?
Fill up her glass! *Versez! versez!*
You see how white are her cheeks to-day.
Sip it, my darling, 'twas ordered for thee;"
He raises his glass, "*À toi Minnie!*"
The *garçon* shuddered, for nothing is there
In the lady's place but an empty chair.

But still with an air of fierce unrest
The vicomte addresses an unseen guest.
" Leave us, Antoine ; we have much to say,
And time is precious to me to-day."
When the *garçon* was gone he sprang up with a start.
" Minié is dead of a broken heart.
Could I think when she gave it with generous joy
A woman's heart such a fragile toy ?
Her trim little figure no longer I see !
Would I were lying with thee, Minié !
For what is life but a hell to me ?
What splendor and wealth but misery ?"
A jet of flame and a whirl of smoke,
A detonation the silence broke.
The landlord enters, and, lying there
Is the dead vicomte, with a stony glare
Rigidly fixed on an empty chair.
Il faut avertir le commissaire !
Ma foi !   Chez Brébant ces choses sont rares.
                5*

TO MY DAUGHTER.

ON HER BIRTHDAY, JULY 27, 1878.

SOLE daughter of my home and heart,
Thy husband's and thy children's love
Will richly crown this happy day ;
Still, from a father's hand receive
An unpremeditated lay.
From heart of mine to heart of thine
It is indeed an humble token,
But yet will whisper of a love
Unspeakable, unspoken,
That deepens with the flight of years—
Receives the baptism of tears,
And gives to life its holiest charm,
To pain and grief the sweetest balm.
All is not lost while I enshrine
Thy image in this heart of mine.
Fate's darkest form I well may bear
While guarded by thy tender care.
May every blessing ever given
Fall on you like the dews of heaven,
And you the happiness you give
In tenfold measure back receive.

SONG.

FROM THE SPANISH OF J. CADALSO.

WHO is it that hither
  Through yon valley trips?
With a bottle in his hand
  And a smile on his lips?
With vines and with ivy
  His temples are crowned;
Fair youths and young maidens
  Encircle him round.
With voice and with timbrel,
  His exploits they laud,
And merrily singing
  His coming applaud.
'Tis Bacchus, the wine god!
  Nay—there you are wrong.
'Tis I, who have written
  This fugitive song.

UNFURL THE FLAG.

I.

UNFURL the flag, our country's flag,
  Upheld by gallant hearts and true—
A star for every sovereign State
  Emblazoned on its field of blue.
No mutilated banner ours
  Of dear-bought honors basely shorn,
With half its glory-beaming stars
  In frenzy from the Union torn.

II.

Lo! like the rainbow on the storm,
  Its colors gild the brow of night,
And proudly dally with the breeze
  As when it gladdened first the sight.
By hero hands that flag was raised,
  When foes around were thickening fast,
And tyrant's power o'er all the land
  Its desolating shadow cast.

III.

When rolled the war-clouds o'er the sky,
   And blazed the lightning fires of death,
That banner met the patriot's eye,
   Who blessed it with his dying breath.
Amid the crash of ocean war,
   High streaming in the sulphury blast,
The flag waved o'er the reeling deck,
   Nailed to the CONSTITUTION's mast.

IV.

Then be it ours to fence from harm
   The glorious flag baptized in flame;
To keep its stars and stripes intact—
   The patriot's pride, the traitor's shame.
Still shall that banner stainless float
   As when in joy and pride unfurled,
Millions of hearts its color-guard,
   The hope of freedom through the world.

SPRING.

An Invitation.

The spring has come—the lovely spring—
   Come, dearest, wander forth with me ;
We'll go where blossoms do not hang
   Upon the sere and leafless tree.

We'll try to find some hardy flower,
   Or some ambitious blade of grass ;
But wear your India-rubbers, love,
   The ice is slippery as glass.

I've got my gutta-percha shoes—
   Warm furs around your shoulders fling,
With cloak, umbrella, and surtout,
   We're fitly dressed to meet the spring.

We'll try and fancy it all right,
   While striding o'er the pastures brown,
We'll say the snow-flakes falling fast
   Are blossomed petals falling down.

When home returning from our walk,
　With noses blue and spirits light,
How gladly will we hover o'er
　The glowing fire of anthracite.

Then come, my love, while the sidewalk's clear,
　Soon will the snow obstruct the way ;
But if this weather only holds
　We'll go a-Maying in a sleigh.

———

ALL.

THERE hangs a sabre, and there a rein,
With a rusty bit and green curb chain ;
A pair of spurs on the old gray wall,
With a mouldy saddle—well, that is all.

Come out to the stable, it is not far,
The moss-grown door is hanging ajar.
Look within, there's an empty stall,
Where once stood a noble horse : that's all.

The good black steed came riderless home,
Flecked with blood-drops as well as foam.
See yonder hillock, where dead leaves fall,
The good black horse pined to death : that's all.

All? Ah, God! it is all I can speak—
Question me not, I am old and weak ;
His saddle and sabre hang on the wall,
His horse pined to death—I have told you all.

THE CAVALRY CHARGE.

WITH bray of the trumpet
 And roll of the drum,
And keen ring of bugle,
 The cavalry come.
Sharp clank the steel scabbards
 The bridle-chains ring,
And foam from red nostrils
 The wild chargers fling.

Tramp ! tramp ! o'er the greensward
 That quivers below,
Scarce held by the curb-bit,
 The fierce horses go ;
And the grim-visaged colonel,
 With ear-rending shout,
Peals forth to the squadrons
 The order—" Trot out ! "

One hand on the sabre,
　And one on the rein,
The troopers move forward
　In line on the plain,
And rings the word "Gallop!"
　The steel scabbards clank,
And each rowel is pressed
　To a horse's hot flank,
And swift is the rush
　As the wild torrent's flow
When it pours from the crag
　On the valley below.

"Charge!" thunders the leader;
　Like shaft from the bow
Each mad horse is hurled
　On the wavering foe.
A thousand bright sabres
　Are gleaming in air,
A thousand dark horses
　Are dashed on the square.

Resistless and reckless
　Of aught may betide,
Like demons, not mortals,
　The wild troopers ride.

Cut right ! and cut left !—
　For the parry who needs !
The bayonets shiver
　Like wind-shattered reeds.

Vain, vain the red volley
　That bursts on the square —
The random-shot bullets
　Are wasted in air.
Triumphant, remorseless,
　Unerring as death—
No sabre that's stainless
　Returns to its sheath.

The wounds that are dealt
　By that murderous steel
Will never yield case
　For the surgeon to heal.
Hurrah ! they are broken !
　Hurrah ! boys, they fly !
None linger save those
　Who but linger to die.

Rein up your hot horses,
　　And call in your men—
The trumpets sound " Rally
　　To color ! " again.
Some saddles are empty,
　　Some comrades are slain,
And some noble horses
　　Lie stark on the plain,
But war's a chance game boys
　　And weeping is vain.

SONG.

Sung at the 222d Anniversary of the Ancient and
Honorable Artillery Co., June 4, 1860.

I.

In the garb that was worn by our fathers of yore,
　　When they sprang from the vales, from the mountains
　　　　descended,
And bearing the arms that they gallantly bore,
　　When their rights and their homes and their lands they
　　　　defended,

We gather to-day,

In martial array,

In the field to parade, at the altar to pray,

And ready in peace and in war to uphold

The Union proclaimed by our fathers of old.

II.

Oh ! dark was the day when our banner uprose,

O'er the fields by the frenzy of battle made gory ;

But sweet and serene was its festival close,

As the stars of our flags glittered forth in their glory.

Forever to be

On land and on sea,

The beacon of nations who dare to be free,

And who look to the hearts and the hands that uphold

The Union proclaimed by our fathers of old.

III.

Fair peace o'er the land of our love reigns supreme,

And long may it be e'er the cannon's deep thunder,

The musketry's flash, and bayonet's gleam,

The veil of repose shall tear rudely asunder.

Yet war's rude appeal
Our strength should reveal,
And call from each scabbard the lightning of steel,
And nerve every heart, every hand to uphold
The Union proclaimed by our fathers of old.

TO HARRY BENNETT.

WRITTEN IN MY GRANDSON'S ALBUM.

Fais ce que dois advienne que pourra.

LIVE for the right, whate'er befall !
  Such living is success,
Whether one's pathway is apart,
  Or crowds around it press,
Whether one meet the sneer of scorn
  Or smile of tenderness.
What if low ignorance and spite
  Your best attempts revile ?
Conscience will tell you what is right,
  What great, what low and vile.
Dear Harry, like a summer sky
  Fortune above you bends,
Youth, health, and strength are yours to-day,
  Kind parents, sister, friends ;

Then be your course through life the course
     That will delight us all ;
Live for the right, for that alone,
     Whatever may befall.

THE PRETTY CIGAR GIRL OF PARIS.

I SIT in my study musing
     And dreaming of things afar,
While the smoke-wreaths are upward curling
     From my fifteen-cent cigar.
And I think of a weed of Paris
     That costs but a single sou ;
Then, maid of the Palais Royal,
     My heart travels backward to you.

The shop I behold with its fixings—
     The counter, the scales, and the till,
The *caporal* done up in papers—
     And ask, are you sitting there still ?
Are your brown, velvet eyes soft as ever ?
     Do they still look a customer through ?
I know that their glances convinced me
     That dark eyes are sweeter than blue.

Are those delicate hands just as snowy,
   A type of the whiteness within,
As when you extended your digits
   And closed them around on my tin ?
I still hear your musical "*Merci !*"
   For coin that was only your due—
Oh ! the heart that would trifle with many
   Would never go back upon you.

Fair faces I've seen by the dozen,
   Impurity framed to conceal ;
But I felt that you formed an exception,
   That *you* never danced at Mabille.
I'd make you my model Madonna,
   If I'd a church painting to do ;
For innocence, sweetness and honor,
   I'd go my whole pile upon you.

You sit in the midst of Havanas,
   A saint in an odorous shrine,
And the dandies that buzz at your counter
   Declare that your charms are divine.
Who knows but your neighbor, Prince Plon-Plon,
   May ply you with soft billet-doux ?
But I am sure that the gas of these ninnies
   Will make no impression on you.

You've smiles for the coxcombs of fashion,
  And yet their allurements you shun ;
You're very bewitching to many,
  But loving and truthful to one.
I saw him—*a chasseur* **à cheval,**
  With pants of the ruddiest hue,
And a great clanking sword, that kept banging
  The **calves** of his legs black and blue.

One day you will go to the *mairié,*
  Then travel again to the church,
Hand in hand with the *chasseur à cheval,*
  Leaving lovers by scores in the lurch.
For muffs that are miffed there's the river,
  When she whom **I** sing about marries,
The maid of the bright Palais Royal,
  The pretty cigar girl of **Paris.**

SOUVENIR DE LUCERNE.

Liebste, sollst mir heute sagen :
  Bist du nicht ein Traumgebild
Wie's in schwülen Sommertagen
  Aus dem Hirn des Dichters quillt ?—HEINE.

I.

WHEREVER my wandering footsteps may turn
I'm sure to remember the Maid of Lucerne—
The maiden I saw by the banks of the Reuss,
So innocent, pretty, inviting and nice.
Wherever my wandering footsteps may turn,
I am sure to remember the Maid of Lucerne.

II.

A trim velvet bodice imprisoned her waist,
An opera ball-room her foot would have graced ;
Her kirtle was scarlet, her stockings were blue,
And a dear little buckle appeared on each shoe.
Wherever my wandering footsteps may turn,
I am sure to remember the Maid of Lucerne.

III.

No *chignon* she wore, but the braids of her hair!
Had a very enticing and *suivez-moi* air.
Her locks were so brown and her eyes were so blue,
That one snared the heart that the others pierced
        through.
Commend me to orbs that can heal if they burn,
And such were the eyes of the Maid of Lucerne.

IV.

She was carrying bricks from her boat to the shore,
By way of a rest from employing the oar ;
And I thought as I saw her, a mortal could stand
A thousand of bricks from so dainty a hand.
Wherever my wandering footsteps may turn,
I shall always remember the Maid of Lucerne.

V.

In a beer-hall at night the maiden I met,
A chopin of lager before her was set ;
But ere on the counter her kreutzers could clink,
I summoned the kellner and paid for the drink,
Receiving sweet gratitude's glance in return
From the azure-blue eyes of the Maid of Lucerne.

THE RHYME OF THE RHINE.

" Wo ich bin,wo ich gehe, mein Hertz ist am Rhein!"—W. MULLER.

I.

A DREAM of enchantment, too quickly 'twas past,
Too lovely its features, too charming to last ;
Field, forest, and mountain, church, castle, and shrine,
Appearing and fleeting—farewell to the Rhine.

II.

What treasures of beauty from Mainz to Cologne !
Oh ! fair is the Danube, and bright is the Rhone,
And lordly the Hudson ; but thou dost combine
All beauties and glories, magnificent Rhine !

III.

The quaint town of Bingen was seen through my tears,
For I thought of that soldier who died in Algiers.
Johannisberg's vines promised plenty of drink,
But only to those who had plenty of chink.

The mortal *sans* **argent** must turn with a tear

From golden-head *Schloss* to the solace of beer.

In Metternich's diggings they've put up a sign :

"If you haven't the rhino, keep clear of the Rhine."

IV.

The old feudal castles, grim, shattered, and brown,

Like rock-rooted eyries look sullenly down,

Through vistas of forest and vistas of vine,

On the glittering sheen of the beautiful Rhine.

V.

The lords of those castles are ashes and dust,

But sleep not exactly the sleep of the just.

They watched for the merchants, and just in the nick

Of time they came down like a thousand of brick ;

And the tradesman who managed to save his own pelt,

By half of his cargo and half of his *gelt*,

With candles and flowers bestowed on a shrine

Gave thanks for achieving his trip down the Rhine.

VI.

No mail-encased noble now troubles your purse,

But landlords and *valets de place* are much worse.

On leaving the former your pittance was small,
On leaving the latter you've nothing at all.
They'll hold you to ransom, demanding a line
On your banker at Paris, these rogues of the Rhine.

VII.

But the glories the banks of the river enfold
Are worth all your discounts of silver and gold.
The dross that you leave to the harpies behind
Is naught to the gems that are stored in your mind :
And to rail at the rubs that you meet on your route
Is something so flat that it's wholly played out ;
And tears fill your eyes, or at least they fill mine,
When you look back and falter, " Farewell to the
Rhine."

APROPOS DES BOTTES.

I.

A PAIR of boots were made for me,
    I vow I thought them quite genteel ;
But one of them, I grieve to say,
    Produced abrasions on my heel.

If he who made them were at hand
   The toe of one he'd surely feel—
How could he make the counter so?
   'Twas certain to abrade my heel.

If that vile snob were only here,
   I'd kick him till I made him squeal;
I'd kick him till he couldn't sit,
   And all for torturing my heel.

In mythic legends there is one
   Whom Frenchmen will miscall Achille;
I take no pride that I, like him,
   Am sorely wounded in the heel.

When I attempt to walk the street
   My limp doth secret pangs reveal,
And every boot-black can perceive,
   Something's the matter with my heel.

Into my old, discarded boot
   My dexter foot slipped like an eel—
Now iron hooks are requisite
   To drag the new one on the heel.

And then I scarcely walk a step
  Before the skin begins to peel ;
I faintly lean against a post
  To ease the anguish of my heel.

In coat of blue and buttons bright,
  Comes one who guards the city's weal,
And says, " My Christian friend, you're tight,"
  The tightness all is in my heel.

His baton to the station-house
  He points, and says to that Bastille
I must directly walk with him.
  Walk ? with that wound upon my heel ?

On either hand an officer—
  I vow 't was vastly ungenteel—
I'm roughly shouldered through the crowd—
  All caused by that confounded heel.

The crowd supposes I've been foiled
  In some insane intent to steal,
And rotten eggs assail my head—
  My head must suffer for the heel.

His honor gently says, "Too thin !"
  When I my hidden woes reveal,
And bids me go and sin no more—
  He don't believe about my heel.

O maker of that cruel boot !
  The cat, the pillory, the wheel
Were punishments too mild for you
  Who tortured thus both head and heel.

Oh ! were we in the days of yore,
  When every gentleman wore steel,
Your carcass through and through I'd bore
  To pay for that abraded heel.

SALUT À LA FRANCE.

Read at the American Dinner at the Grand Hôtel, Paris,
July 4, 1872.

While to your banner gemmed with stars
  Our eyes are turned with rapture's glance,
We hail alike with beating hearts,
  The friendly flag of France.

And till those hearts have ceased to throb,
  'Till freedom's latest sun has set,
The name of Washington will blend
  With that of Lafayette.

Aye, long as history holds a scroll,
  Or place for one recorded line,
For scenes of triumph and of toil,
  Yorktown and Brandywine.

And where, when we have left our land
  A thousand weary leagues away,
Could we more fitly congregate
  To celebrate this day

Than here, where friendly hearts and hands
  A welcome give where'er we turn,
Where souls with kindred hopes are fired,
  With kindred raptures burn?

Breathe but the word " American,"
  The hearts of Paris wide expand;
And he of us who loved not France
  Would spurn his native land,

Turn from the memory of his sires,
　　Forget the gratitude they bore
To those who battled in their ranks
　　In the stern days of yore.

To know the sons of this fair land,
　　To read their story is to trace
The deeds of an heroic age,
　　Of a chivalric race.

Their path through sunshine and through shade
　　Has waked the wonder of the world ;
Whether they drew the hero's sword,
　　Or war's torn banner furled.

Science and art their victories
　　Have blazoned on their nation's shield ;
The pen, the pencil, and the blade
　　'Tis theirs alike to wield.

And still, upon the height of fame
　　Shall we behold their proud advance,
Like eagles soaring to the sun,
　　Their *salut à la France !*

ON THE SEA BEACH.

HOARSE and exulting,
  Raving and swirling,
Boiling and seething,
  Foaming and whirling;
Raking the pebbles,
  Harsh and discordant,
Gnawing the boulders,
  Venomous, mordant;
Gorged to repletion,
  Craving for more,
Back rolls the bellowing
  Tide from the shore.

Yet was its task-work
  Faithfully done;
Yet were its laurels
  Loyally won.
Bedded in seaweed,
  Cradled in sand,
Waifs of the ocean
  Claimed by the land;

Fairer than marble,
   Colder than clay,
Dewed by baptismal
      Drops of the spray.

Just where the rollers
      Cease to invade,
There were two children,
      Tenderly laid.
Two little hands
      Linked in each other,
Two little angels,
      Sister and brother.
Lilies in purity,
      Cherubs in form,
Waifs from the death-wreck,
      Trophies of storm.

Father and mother,
      Say, where are they?
Saved from the surges
      Thirsting for prey,

Saved to behold
    What the ocean has landed,
Saved to deplore
    What the billows have stranded,
. Saved to be hitherward
        Wandering led ?
God, in his mercy,
    Grant they are dead.

THE CREWLESS SHIP.

The following lines were founded on a singular circumstance which occurred on the shores of Rhode Island in the year 1760. The facts are related without coloring in the poem. The mystery has never been cleared up.

'TWAS a fine autumnal morning,
    And the mist had cleared away,
When a ship with all her canvas spread
    Neared Narragansett Bay.

With all her canvas spread—
    'Twas a glorious sight I ween
To mark her in the freshening blast
    Low to the wave careen.

The foam she flung right gallantly,
    Like flower-wreaths, far and free,
And her topsail yards by the mast inclined—
    They almost kissed the sea.

With a sound like rushing pinions
    She swiftly ploughed her way,
A gallant, glorious messenger
    For Narragansett Bay !

The Islanders on Newport beach
    Her graceful form descry,
And scan her fluttering signal flag
    Like a sea-bird in the sky.

"'Tis the bark from merrie England !"
    So rang the cheering cry ;
'Twas joyous news to many a heart
    That she was drawing nigh.

The wife, so long a watcher
    For the partner of her heart,
The fond and plighted maiden
    Played well the woman's part.

With tearful eyes, o'ershaded
　By trembling hands, they mark
The fast enlarging vision;
　The tall and shapely bark !

But lo ! a cry of terror
　From the crowd upon the shore !
The ship is fast approaching
　Where the angry surges roar.

To right and left the sunken rocks
　Resist the billows' force—
Why sternly holds the vessel on
　The same unvaried course ?

Why heeds she not the warning
　That rises from the beach
When shelving rocks are thundering
　Far as the eye can reach ?

Right onward, like a phantom ship
　Or the mirage of the sea—
Rising and plunging heavily
　Due shoreward rushes she.

Where sleeps the hand whose duty
   It is to grasp the helm ?
If she holds on her doom is sealed—
   The waves her crew o'erwhelm.

Nearer and nearer yet !
   The bravest hearts on land
Throb hard with horror at the sight !
   The vessel strikes the strand !

They board her—on her slippery deck
   No human form is found ;
They call aloud—no human voice
   Gives answer to the sound.

Above, below they search in vain—
   No trace of life is there—
And the loved who looked for loved ones home
   Are destined to despair.

And whether, in a nameless fear
   Of danger and of wreck,
They quitted for an open boat
   The fastness of the deck,

Or murder red and mutiny
   Were busy with the knife,
And gallant hearts had throbbed their last
   In treason's deadly strife,

We may not hear or know until
   The sea gives up its dead,
And earth's vast crew shall summoned rise
   Before their Captain dread.

But still the everlasting sea
   Rolls onward as before,
And still upon the shining sand
   The curving surges roar.

And still the Island mariners
   To list'ners love to teach
The story of the "Crewless Ship"
   Once wrecked on Newport beach.

THE LANCER OF THE GUARD.

I SIT at the close of an autumn day
Where a white fountain throws up its spray,
Half screened by many a red-brown tree
Lies the ruined front of the Tuileries,
And, mistily sketched on the sky's blue field,
Rise the open towers of Sainte-Clotilde,
With a gleam of gold from the massive dome
That marks the site of the soldier's home,
Where the greatest of captains lies at rest
In the spot of earth that he loved the best ;
And far away, up the avenue,
Distant and cloud-like in airy hue,
The Arch that tells of triumphs won
Sweeps like a frame round the setting sun.
All about me the children play
As if life were only a holiday.

But who comes halting by on a crutch ?
A wreck of war—I thought as much.
Carefully steps he over the ground,
Then halts and wistfully looks around,

With a weary air, as one would do
Too early or late for a rendezvous.
Touched by his sad and lonely air,
I offered the haggard man a chair.
" Thanks, monsieur," and he takes the seat,
" Young as I am, repose is sweet.
Once I could join in the merry dance—
Mais n'importe! I lost my leg for France.
For a limb the less need a soldier care ?
C'est à la guerre, comme à la guerre !
Sometimes I think with a passing pain,
I never must sit in saddle again,
Nor draw a sabre or level a lance
When the trumpet rallies the sons of France.

" We were many in days of yore,
With hearts as light as the plumes we wore ;
Even the Emperor's dull, cold eye
Lighted up as we thundered by,
A scurrying mass of azure and steel,
With shouts that rang out like the musket's peal.

" We were many in days of yore,
Comrades true to the warm heart's core,

Friends in revel and friends in fray,
Life to us was a carnival day.
And I might have been a *mauvais sujet*
But one fine day it was here I met
The girl of my heart—my Antoinette ;
Then I could walk, and dance and ride,
And light was my step at my darling's side.

" But war and love are enemies sworn,
Away from the girl of my heart I was torn—
No time for wooing when sabres shine !
War ! war ! for the German had crossed the Rhine.

" We were many who rode to the front
To take our share of the battle's brunt,
We were few who came home again
When the blood of France had been poured in vain.

" Love-making adieu ! for Beauty's mate
Is a man complete—not a thing whom Fate
Has marked for life, and so carved and torn,
That better he never had been born."

He rises, he smiles, and takes my hand,—
"Spare me your pity, you see I can stand.

Merci, monsieur ; but I must not stay,
She I expected is coming this way,
For the crippled lancer there's joy in life,
Since Antoinette is his loving wife ! "

THE FAIRY BOTTINES.

A LEGEND OF THE SPLENDIDE HÔTEL.

A DEAR little pair of gaiters—
   The instep had such a swell !—
Were placed at the door just opposite
   To mine in the Splendide Hôtel.

For the feet of a Cinderella,
   The feet of a fairy belle,
Was surely designed that *chaussure*
   I saw at the Splendide Hôtel.

When the hour of nine was sounded
   From the tongue of clock and bell,
The hand of an angel dropped those boots
   In the hall of the Splendide Hôtel.

The hand, like the **foot**, was *mignonne*,
　　And the beauty what tongue could tell
Of the doubtless divine *incognita*
　　Who lived at the Splendide Hôtel.

At the hour of ten in the morning
　　Abruptly vanished the spell,
And the little *bottines* disappeared
　　From the hall of the Splendide Hôtel.

What was the name of the fair one ?
　　Was it Marie or Annabelle ?
I would not enquire of Madeleine,
　　Who waits at the Splendide Hôtel.

Those **bottines looked very** lonely—
　　If I'd been a younger swell,
I should surely have sought the acquaintance
　　Of the sylph of the Splendide Hôtel.

But scattered were all my illusions
　　By a sight that may well dispel
The wildest dream of a poet
　　Who lived at the Splendide Hôtel.

By the side of the bottines one morning—
  What tongue can the horror tell?—
Stood a pair of the hugest cowhide boots
  Ever seen at the Splendide Hôtel.

The owner of boots so atrocious
  Had braved the Atlantic swell,
And arrived in the month of December
  Safe and sound at the Splendide Hôtel.

The garçon told me his legend,
  While blacking those boots pell-mell—
They reached from the second story
  To the third of the Splendide Hôtel.

He said that the wretch was married,
  That he owned a petroleum well,
And his bride had preceded him thither,
  And stopped at the Splendide Hôtel.

The garçon and I united
  In wishing the monster—well,
At a place located much farther
  Away than the Splendide Hôtel.

I had but one glance at the being,
　As he stood on the street next day,
His heels in the Place de l' Opera,
　His toes in the Rue de la Paix.

And she was smiling beside him
　Who had made my dream a sell,
Who had bartered her peerless charms for " ile,"
　And lived at the Splendide Hôtel.

I entered the smoking-room wildly,
　And savagely rang the bell,
And paid my bill and started for Rome,
　Away from the Splendide Hôtel.

SERENADE.

WAKE, lady, wake! the starry eyes
    Of heaven their nightly vigils keep ;
Then why should beauty's brighter orbs
    Be vailed in envious sleep'?

Here, along the winding paths,
    Where evening hides their rainbow bloom,
The flowers you love give up to-night
    Their sweetest, best perfume.

Then from your lattice kindly bend
    One moment to survey the scene,
That lacks the loveliest ornament—
    The presence of Claudine.

Let me but gaze on that loved form—
    'Tis all my wishes dare desire,
Then he who all unknown adores
    Will silently retire.

7

THE MAN IN GRAY.

A Simple and True Story.

His name, if ever known, has passed away ;
We only knew him as the " Man in Gray ; "
Men shrugged their shoulders when he came,
And hinted that his wits had gone astray.
Yet will his deeds be entered on that scroll
That holds the record of each human soul.
Poorly, but neatly clad, he came and went,
Always on deeds of charity intent—
Begging each one he met to give " one cent."
The rich, by Heaven endowed with bounteous store,
Would fain have made his humble scrip flow o'er.
But, no ! Let each the smallest coin bestow—
So shall we lift the load of human woe.
'Tis grains of sand that build the mountain high—
Atoms, combined, create infinity.
Such were his thoughts, and so the Man in Gray,
Begging for others, went his weary way;
The gathered mites sufficed to buy a store
Of medicine, of food—he sought no more.

The fever patient knew his gentle face ;
Beside the couch of pain there was his place ;
And when the ransomed spirit passed away
What prayers were murmured by the Man in Gray !
To crippled children, reft of childhood's joys,
The Man in Gray brought flowers and books and toys.
So, all through life, the nameless hero trod
The Saviour's footpath leading up to God.

Learn from his simple life, we all have power
To help our fellows in misfortune's hour.
The wealth of trifles in the bitter day
Was demonstrated by the Man in Gray.

OH, WHY ARE THE ROSES SO PALE?

TRANSLATED FROM THE GERMAN OF HEINRICH HEINE.

Oh, why are the roses so pale, my love ?
    Can'st tell me the reason why ?
And why in the depths of the grassy grove
    Does the violet shrink from the eye ?

And why has the lark such a querulous lay—
   As he soars to the sky from the heath ?
And why do the flowers that grow by the way
   Exhale such an odor of death ?

And why is the sunlight so wan and austere
   That fields are enshrouded in gloom ?
And why is the bosom of earth so sere
   That it looks to the eye like a tomb?

And why do I feel such a sickness at heart
   By a conflict of agony torn ?
The answer, then, dearest, adored one, impart,
   Oh, why hast thou left me forlorn ?

LAFAYETTE.

IF ever sainted spirits leave
   The limits of their blissful sphere,
Lafayette! we may well believe
   That thine to-day is hovering near.
When memories of the past arise—
   The storm of war, the charging line,
The stars and lilies side by side,
   Yorktown and Brandywine,

None braver than those men of old
   E'er wielded blade or levelled lance—
Our country's hardy yeomanry,
   The chivalry of France.

Dear wert thou to our "chief of men,"
   His brother, friend, adopted son;
Who thinks of thee but he recalls
   Our deathless Washington?

Fresh from the sculptor's cunning hand,
   Thy form with reverence we behold—
Gift of thy liberated land,
   Dearer than molten gold.

Living thou wert the link to bind
   Our country to thy beauteous land;
The bond thy memory consecrates
   Intact shall ever stand.

Long as our mountains kiss the sky
   And in the sun our rivers glance,
Our hearts in gratitude and love
   Shall proudly turn to France.

Ne'er again may despot's sway
   Her soaring aspirations foil!
Never again invading foot
   Tread on her verdant soil!

From Liberty's advancing form

    Be every shadow backward cast !

And let the purest, brightest wreath

    Rest on her brows at last !

September 6.

————

LINES WRITTEN AT SEA.

" Though his bark may not be lost,
    Still it may be tempest tost."—SHAKESPEARE.

THE sky is as black as a sky can well be,

But murkier yet is the thundering sea ;

Loud roars through the rigging the fierce winter gale

And smites in its fury the double-reefed sail.

We mount o'er the billows we cannot divide,

And sweep from the crests down the watery slide.

From starboard to port we are saucily tost,

A boom like a gun and the topsail is lost !

Blown clear from the bolt-ropes to leeward it flies—

But onward the dauntless *Westphalia* hies.

The spirits of storm may their uttermost do—

The good German steamer will carry us through.

The lights, like a monster's unwavering eyes,

Glare scorn at the fury of billows and skies ;

The Vision of Death may arise in our way,

But the Giant of Fire will carry the day.

That giant we've tamed to the veriest slave,

And the might of his toil has the power to save.

He roars in his den and the thunders of steel,

Like the clashing of weapons, his powers reveal.

Look down through the hatchways ! Dark forms to and fro

Are reeling to-night, and their fires are aglow.

There are serpent-like hisses and gushes of steam,

Foul stenches and clangor and glamour and gleam !

Keep the stokers at work ! On the deck Captain Stahl,

Firm braced on his bridge, holds a watch over all !

Three stout sons of Germany stand at the wheel

And grip to the spokes as with vises of steel.

Keep the ship on her course, with her head to the wind,

The savage Atlantic his mistress shall find ;

For the battle he covets to us is but sport

While the gallant Westphalia bears us to port.

ANDREAS HOFER.

TRANSLATED FROM THE GERMAN OF JULIUS MOSEN.

Andreas Hofer, the "**Tell of the Tyrol**," defended the mountain passes of his native land against the **French, in 1809**, with **heroic** bravery. He was betrayed into the hands of a French general, tried and sentenced by court-martial, at Mantua, and shot February **20, 1810**. His son was ennobled by the Emperor of Austria ; and **his body lies** in the splendid Cathedral of Innspruck.

AT Mantua, in fetters,
　Heroic Hofer lay ;
The foe, to death, in Mantua,
　Had carried him away.
Each brother's heart with anguish **bled—**
In Germany what tears were **shed,**
　And Tyrol's mountain land !

With hands behind him folded,
　Unshaken, hand and limb,
He marched with steady **footsteps,**
　For what was death to him ?
Death, which his hand, in leaden hail
Had oft hurled downward on the vale
　In Tyrol's holy land.

When, from the prison-grating,

    The mountaineer's keen eye

Had seen his brother riflemen

    Hold up their hands on high,

He prayed that God would give them aid,

And bless poor Germany betrayed,

    And Tyrol, land adored.

No stirring martial drum-beat

    Was there to time the march

As forth Andreas Hofer

    Moved from the dungeon's arch.

There, on the frowning bastion, he,

In spite of chains, stood spirit-free,

    Tyrol's heroic son ;

And said, when told that he must kneel :

    " My knee I will not bend,

But stand as I have stood and fought,

    Nor crouch to meet my end ;

Unveiled, behold the lightning glance

Of Death.   Long live my emperor, Franz,

    And Tyrol's mountain land."

    7*

The bandage to a grenadier
   He gave, and, undismayed,
The hero, for a moment's space,
   In silent fervor prayed.
Then shouted, " Fire ! " Forth leaped the flame,
" Ah ! " he exclaimed ; " how ill you aim.
   Dear Tyrol, fare thee well ! "

DRIFTING.

My bark drifts over a soundless sea,
While the untrimmed sails flap wearily,
And her timbers yield a painful moan
That answers the gray sea's undertone,
Wrinkled and gray, as I have grown.

Listless I lie on the mouldy deck,
Heedless if drifting to port or wreck,
Never a hand to the wheel I lift
But suffer the worn old bark to drift,
Whether the wind blow high or low,
Or the subtle current and undertow
Draw her on with resistless guile
To the fatal reefs of a coral isle.

For whether I lie in the ruthless sea,
Or in sacred earth my slumbers be,
Is matter of small account to me.

For the light of life is quenched and gone,
And a pall hangs over the noonday sun,
And the once-loved song of the summer sea
Rings like a knell from the billows free.

The light of my life was from kindly eyes,
That every morn were a glad surprise,
And the chiming song of the summer sea
Owed all of its winning minstrelsy
To the joyous laugh that came with the breath
Of lips that are sealed in steadfast death.
A human life was the golden key
Of nature's limitless treasury.

So by the useless helm I sit,
While the drifting shadows fail and flit
Over the web of the dusky sail,
As clouds are driven by breeze or gale,
And even the sun on the pulseless sea
Shines with no golden light for me.

ABD-EL-KADER AND NAPOLEON III.

TRANSLATED FROM THE FRENCH OF VICTOR HUGO.*

" The Emir himself looked no unworthy leader of such a host. His keen eye glittered like a falcon's under the snowy hood which threw his war-worn face into deep shadow. His nervous, wiry figure, of which the muscular proportions were scarcely concealed by the loose, white garments that drooped about him, sat erect upon his lofty, cumbrous saddle, unlike those of his chiefs, ornamented only by a border of seed pearls embroidered on its velvet housings. His black mare, with her clean, small head and scarlet nostrils, arched her foam-flecked neck, as she champed and fretted on a powerful bit under the loose rein and light touch of her rider's hand. A cord of twisted tissue, striped like a serpent's skin, secured the hood of the Emir's burnouse ; a sharp sabre hung, edge uppermost, at his belt. Save these, arms and ornaments he had none ! Yet the Englishman, scanning that white-draped figure on the good black mare, standing out from the array of Arab chivalry, apart and by itself, wondered no longer at the Emir's ascendency over his people, at their heroic and unreasoning devotions to one, in whom, like a second Mahomet, they believed as warrior, priest, and king."—G. J. WHYTE MELVILLE.

WHEN Abd-el-Kader, from his cell,
  Beheld the small-eyed man advance
Whom History and whom Troplong call
  Napoleon Third of France ;

* Written by the French poet soon after the infamous and bloody *coup d'etat* of December 2, 1852.

Saw, coming to his dungeon-grate,
　Close followed by his servile band,
Th' Elysee's dull and squint-eyed man ;
　He of the desert's sand,

He, sultan born, beneath the palms,
　Playmate of lions huge and wild,
The Hadji, with his calm dark eyes,
　The Emir, fierce yet mild ;

He, pitiless as Fate itself,
　Riding, white-robed with spectral glare,
Now, drunk with carnage, spurring forth,
　Then kneeling low in prayer ;

Who flinging wide his canvas tent,
　And bending 'neath the evening star,
Feared not to lift in reverence
　His hands blood-red with war ;

Who gave the sword its draught of blood,
　Yet, with a mystic, dreaming eye,
Throned on a pile of human heads,
　Surveyed the beauteous sky ;

Seeing the treacherous, cunning look,
    The low brow with its brand of shame,
He, splendid soldier, glorious priest,
    Asked who it was that came ?

Who was this base mustachio'd mask
    He knew not,—but they told him—"See !
The lictors with their axes pass—
    The bandit Cæsar he !

" List, Emir, to these mournful wails—
    This clamor rising from the dust ;
This man by mothers is reviled,
    By woman's tongue is cursed.

" He makes them widows—rends their hearts—
    France by his traitor hand is dead,
And now he gnaws her body."   Then
    The Emir bowed his head.

But loathing in his heart the rogue
    In whom he knew all vices blent,
The tiger's nostril in disdain
    Turned from the wolf's vile scent.

VORWAERTS! IMMER VORWAERTS!

On, still on ! the ground is quaking
    With the cannon's thunder-roll,
Never daunting, never shaking
    Germany's heroic soul.
Does the river, from the mountain
    Launched with a resistless force,
Refluent, seek its native fountain
    Pouring backward in its course ?

Backward ! 'Tis a word unspoken
    In the language of the North.
Till the opposing force be broken
    Still the tide must thunder forth ;
Tossing high its plumy billows,
    Over mountain, over plain,
Onward, to where Paris pillows
    Her fair head beside the Seine.

But no more the Siren, sleeping,
    Dreams in sloth her hours away,
Clad in mail a watch she's keeping
    Ready for the fiery fray.

Now she bids her cannon utter
  Words of no uncertain sound,
Hopes she by her breath to flutter
  Hearts like those who close her round?

Cannonade and furious sally
  Heaping the broad field with slain,
Charging column, desperate rally,
  Deeds of glory—all are vain.
For the shadow on the dial
  Never wavers, never waits ;
Lonely in her hour of trial,
  She must open wide her gates.

Hers the hand that loosed the torrent,
  Hers the breast to feel the blow ;
She must quaff, howe'er abhorrent,
  To its dregs the cup of woe.
Happy still if she discover
  How the future may be won,
And the might, the wide world over,
  Of the brave words : "On, still on !"

DEATH AND LIFE.

A FUNERAL train, with solemn pace and slow,
   Moved through the street, nor paused the idle throng
To mark the common pageantry of woe,
   Or ask what shrouded form was borne along.

In that procession I alone descried
   A winged angel who, with drooping head,
Keeping his place the shrouded hearse beside,
   Moved o'er the pavement with a noiseless tread.

The sculptured cemetery-gate at last
   Threw its deep shadow on the halted train ;
Its dark brown leaves appeared securely fast,
   The angel smote once, twice, and again.

Then from within a voice of silver tone,
   Of a strange, thrilling melody possessed,
Asked, in a tongue to all but me unknown,
   "Whom is it thou bring'st hither ? "   " A still guest."

"What is it that he seeks?"   "He seeks repose."

    "The rest *I* give is dreamless," said the Unseen ;

"My gates to every mortal must unclose—

    Gates which the House of Silence shield and screen."

Noiseless the portal opened.   Forth there came

    A second angel, and I held my breath,

For on his brow there burned a wreath of flame,

    It was Azrael, angel crowned of Death !

And he who walked beside the bier,

    Angel of Life.   So each the other clasped,

And neither smiled, and neither shed a tear,

    As through the gate the funeral convoy passed.

The angels met and parted at the portal,

    None saw their mute embrace and mute farewell,

Or knew what Spirits welcomed an Immortal,

    And mourned not, for they knew that all was well.

GOOD-NIGHT.

ALL alone on the wrathful ocean,
Cold and black in its fierce commotion !
Where is the bark with its pennon gay,
That bore us to sea on a summer day,
With sun-gilt sails and a merry crew,
Above and below a field of blue ?
Where are the lips that laughed and sang
As over the billows our vessel sprang ?

The wild cyclone rent every sail,
The spars were lost in the savage gale,
The waters rose and the waters fell,
Crushing to pieces the feeble shell.
Never a friendly sail in sight !
The man-eating shark sups well to-night,
And I, alone in my agony,
Swimming for life on the midnight sea.

Oh, for a plank ! Oh, for an oar !
To die so near to the destined shore !

Yet why should I live ?   Why struggle on
When they who made life a boon are gone ?
But, look ! a star, like an angel's eye,
Beams through a rift in the cloven sky.

Brighter than jewel in diadem,
It shines like the Star of Bethlehem ;
Over foaming wave-crest and desperate hollow
Its silver pathway is that I must follow.
Muscle and sinew be true to your lord,
And save me to-night from a death abhorred !
Give me, fair star, but thy radiance bright,
I will not be food for the shark to-night.

Quenched and gone ! it is starless now,
A circle of iron is binding my brow ;
My pulse is faint, my senses swim,
And weary, how weary is every limb !
And, sharper than death, through the waters dark
I hear the rush of the fin-back shark.
Never my footsteps shall press the shore,
I go to those who have gone before ;
Horror and storm—not a ray of light !
Terrible world, Good-night ! Good-night !

EDWIN FORREST.

THE curtain falls.   The drama of life
   Is ended.   One who trod the mimic stage
As if the crown, the sceptre, and the robe
   Were his by birthright—worn from youth to age—
"Aye, every inch a king," with voiceless lips,
Lies in the shadow of Death's cold eclipse.

Valete et plaudite !   Well might he
   Have used the Roman language of farewell,
Who was the "noblest Roman of them all;"
   For Brutus spoke and Coriolanus fell,
And Spartacus defied the she-wolf's power
In the great actor's high meridian hour.

How as the noble Moor he wooed and wed
   His bride of Venice ; how his o'erwrought soul,
Tortured and racked and wildly passion tossed,
   Was whirled, resisting, to the fatal goal,
Doting, yet dooming !   Every trait was true ;
He lived the king the poet drew.

Room for the aged Cardinal! Once more
  The greatest statesman France has ever known
Waked from the grave and wove his subtle spells;
  A power behind, but greater than the throne.
Is Richelieu gone? It seems but yesterday
We heard his voice and saw his features play.

Greatest of all in high creative skill
  Was Lear, poor, discrowned king and hapless sire.
What varied music in the actor's voice!
  The sigh of grief, the trumpet tone of ire.
Now both are hushed; we ne'er shall hear that strain
Of well-remembered melody again.

No fading laurels did his genius reap;
  With Shakespeare's best interpreters full high
His name is graven on Fame's temple front,
  With Kean's and Kemble's, names that will not die
While memory venerates the poet's shrine
And holds his music more than half divine.

ONWARD.

Nor look nor footstep backward turn,
  Though many a vanished scene be fair ;
There's less nepenthe in the urn
  Of memory than despair.
The future we can carve at will—
  The sculptured past defies our skill.

Why summon up the weird array
  Of spectres false—Delusion's train ?
The idols time has proved of clay
  Will ne'er be gold again :
Nor deft alchemy restore
  The treasures that we prized of yore.

Onward life's river boldly pours—
  And when we've won the skill to guide
Then enginery of sails and oars,
  Why backward cleave the tide ?
If beauty charmed the vanished scene,
  We'll look to find some new Undine.

The wreaths that decked our youthful brows
 Have lost their brightness and perfume :
We'll weave our crowns from fresher boughs
 And flowers of richer bloom.
And brighter sunbeams than of old
Shall change our sails to molten gold.

We will not think of reef or wreck,
 Of latent dangers hurried o'er,
Of storms that whilom swept our deck,
 Our Pharos shines before,
And gilds the waves that ceaseless sweep
On the vast, eternal deep.

THE LOVELY FISHERMAIDEN.

TRANSLATED FROM **THE GERMAN OF** HEINRICH HEINE.

THOU lovely fishermaiden,
 Come row thy boat to land,
And sit thee down beside me,
 We'll whisper, hand-in-hand.

Thy head upon my bosom,
 Fear not, my child, to rest,
Dost thou not frolic daily
 With the ocean's heaving breast ?

My heart is like that ocean
With its stormy ebb and flow,
And hides full many a priceless pearl
Within its depths below.

THE OLD CORPORAL.

TRANSLATED FROM THE FRENCH OF BÉRANGER.

MARCH, comrades, march—the hour has come—
With shouldered arms and bearing steady !
You've my discharge within your guns,
My time is up and I am ready.
I've lingered in the ranks too long,
Grown gray in camp and battle ; still
I loved you, lads, and liked to teach
The manual of arms and drills.

Conscripts, don't weep—
But mark ! step keep !
Right foot ! step keep !

A beardless boy insulted me—
Think you his epaulettes I saw ?
I cut him down ! He's getting well ;
I die—for that is martial law.

8

Brandy and passion did their work,
   To vengeance I was hurried on ;
Pride—honor—how could I forget
   When I had served Napoleon?
         Conscripts, don't weep—
         But mark ! step keep !
         Right foot ! step keep !

Conscripts, **you'll never have** the chance
   To win the cross that valor **brings ;**
I got mine in those wars of old,
   Those wars in which we hustled kings.
You've paid the drinks when I have told
   Of battles fierce in sand and snow
Of Egypt, Russia, and **the rest ;**
   But what avail **is glory now ?**
         Conscripts, **don't** weep—
         But mark ! step keep !
         Right foot ! step keep !

Robert, you left my native town—
   Go back and tend your father's sheep.
Yon trees are green, but greener far
   Our forests in their endless sweep.

How oft I've ranged our woodland glades
  When leaves and moss with dews were wet.
This hour their memory bright revives!
  There my old mother's living yet !
     Conscripts, don't weep
     But mark ! step keep !
     Right foot ! step keep!

What woman's sobbing then ? I know—
  The drummer's widow. Far away
In Russia, in the rear-guard ranks
  I bore her baby night and day ;
And but for me, the babe and she
  A sepulchre of snow had known.
Kind heart ! my soul will have her prayers
  Ere many minutes past have flown.
     Conscripts, don't weep—
     But mark ! step keep !
     Right foot ! step keep.

The deuce ! my pipe is out at last !
  We've reached the spot ! How fast time flies !
Now, comrades, take aim steadily !
  Don't tie that rag about my eyes !

Sorry to trouble you so much !
  Just one word more—don't fire too low !
A safe returns to happy homes !
  Good-night ! It's time for me to go !
      Conscripts, don't weep—
      But mark ! step keep !
      Right foot ! step keep !

THE HUSSAR AND HIS HORSE.

TRANSLATED FROM THE HUNGARIAN.

PALE, faint, upon the moonlit grass
  A wounded Magyar lay,
While like a trickling rivulet
  His life-blood ebbed away.

He looked upon his faithful steed,
  Who stood with drooping head—
His loyal servant through the war—
  And bitter tears he shed.

And must we part, old comrade, friend ?
  Thou wilt have sorry fare
Within Vienna's hated walls—
  The water's brackish there.

The hay is bitter.   In the stall
　　Thou'lt look in vain for me,
And how can I repose in peace
　　My beauty without thee ?

Before thy bound, before my blade,
　　The savage foe went down ;
And can'st thou bear the galling weight
　　Of some barefooted clown ?

He kissed his horse, he petted him,
　　His memory all ablaze,
Even as the rainbow gilds the storm,
　　Brought thoughts of happier days.

'Tis better that we should not part—
　　Together we have striven—
They'll want us up above to hunt
　　The Germans out of heaven.

And when the skies are clear of them,
　　The brave Hussar perforce,
Must keep pace with the lightning's flash ;
　　In Heaven he needs his horse.

He snatched his sabre, thrust it deep
    Within his horse's heart ;
Their life-blood flowed in blended streams—
    They would not, could not part.

And down upon the battle-field
    Gazed silent moon and star,
Where lay in death the faithful horse
    Beside the dead Hussar.

AUTUMN.

CAN this be death with all this pageantry,
These treasures of a wondrous alchemy,
Leaves changed to gold, and disks of dusky brown
To flakes of crimson, touched with quivering fire ?
This is no funeral, but a coronation—
Nature renounces Death.   The heralds cry :
" The king is dead," but add : " Long live the king ! '
Her throne is never vacant.   Now she writes,
In jewelled hieroglyphs, her proud " Resurgam." *
These gems of vivid color that surround us
Breathe not defeat, but victory ; a triumph

* I shall rise again.

O'er the pallid, scowling King of Terrors.
There's no such thing as death, only a halt
In the relentless march of Time, while wide
The gates of gold are flung before the hosts
Innumerable, ever moving onward,
Upward, also to Eternal Life.

IN MEMORY OF JAMES OAKES.

"A man so sterling and true that his friendship was a consecration
like the Cross of the Legion of Honor."—*New York Evening Express.*

BENEATH the verdant sod and whispering trees,
His requiem sweetly sung by bird and breeze ;
Like the true friend of many changeful years,
Serene and sad, of laughter and of tears.
The joy was brighter, grief less hard to bear,
With his warm sympathy in both to share.
When the death-angel visited my door,
And, one by one, away my treasures bore,
His voice it was that taught me how to bear
The weight of sorrow and defy despair.
The harshest critic might his record scan,
Nor could deny him this—He was a man !

Aye, every inch a man, true, generous, brave,

Steadfast in friendship to the closing grave ;

In health, in sickness, in the parting hour,

He never bowed to Wealth, or cringed to Power.

Friend of the friendless, to the suffering poor

His aid, unasked, was liberal and sure ;

No ostentatious aid—in secret given—

Forgotten here, but registered in Heaven.

Thousands his manly virtues will attest,

And bathe with tears his lovely place of rest.

Those who best knew him were those who loved him best.

June 12, 1878.

"LOOK IN THY HEART AND WRITE."

Thus did'st thou, Sir Philip Sydney,

Teach the secret of all art.

Printed page, illumined missal

Do but weary lore impart ;

Echo not another's fancies,

Be the artist of thy heart.

Sculptor ! not in venal model

Wilt thou beauty's image find ;

Rather seek the bright ideal

In thy heart of hearts enshrined ;
Lines of nature, lines of fancy,
  In a wondrous whole combined.

Painter ! memories of sunsets
  Kindling earth, and air, and sea ;
Springtime's promise, autumn's glory,
  Must thy inspiration be,
Thence the magic evolution
  Of a master's royalty.

Study, poet, study ever,
  But th' unwritten Book of Life,
Nature's tome that holds forever
  Joy and sorrow, peace and strife.

Ponder well its many lessons,
  Take them to thy inmost soul.
Would'st thou see the world enchanted ?
  Then unfold the precious scroll.

Keep not back one bright impression,
  Not one inspiration smother ;
Make thy poem a confession
  And each man will be thy brother.
  8*

FOR THE KING !

THE lady of Ashleigh has armed her good lord,
To heel and to waist buckled fast spur and sword,
Across his broad shoulders his baldric has cast,
And brings him a cavalry-guidon at last.
"This poor little flag I have 'broidered for thee,
With the crown and the sceptre in gold thread you see ;
Let it float in the van when the welkin shall ring
With the Cavaliers' thundering "Long live the King!"

"One kiss, noble wench, ere I ride to the fray ;
The Roundheads shall know me and feel me to-day,
If Old Noll is there the wild echoes shall ring
As the stout men of Ashleigh strike home 'For the
        King !' "

The tenants of Ashleigh were loyal and leal ;
The court-yard was filling with scarlet and steel,
And stout old Sir Christopher, bravest and best,
Spurred out of the gate in advance of the rest.

The lady of Ashleigh is kneeling in prayer,
While the mutter of battle is filling the air;
As each breeze brings the shudder of death on its wing
She prays for Sir Christopher—prays for the King.

The darkness is deep, and the hour is late
When the tramp of a war-horse is heard at the gate;
In his saddle the rider is sitting erect,
But ah! with what stain his bright armor is flecked!
"I am faint. Quick! a goblet of Burgundy bring!"
He raises the cup and he drinks to the King.

"Here's your color, my lass; there are stains on its
    shine—
Some blood of the rebels, and some blood of mine.
Your cup has revived me, 'twas excellent wine.
When the last clod of earth on my coffin they fling,
Let them know, dearest Lilian, I—*died*—for the King!"

ITALY.

Tell me not it was all a dream,
    Wrought out of Fancy's falsest ties,
That we have basked beneath the gleam
    Of Italy's unrivalled skies.

At Venice did we watch on high
　　The moon and stars in glittering march,
Emerging in our gondola
　　From the Rialto's midnight arch ?
Did we not see the sudden storm
　　Sweep down the crested Apennines
Blunting within its murky folds
　　The lances of the waving pines ?

Did we not in eternal Rome
　　Behold, as Art enchained our breath,
The triumph of the molten bronze,
　　The gladiator's deathless death ?
And Naples—color, life, and light,
　　Pompeii, Baia, and Capri.
Vesuvius, glowing through the night—
　　These did we dream or did we see ?
Florence the fair and Genoa,
　　Milan, Marengo's battle-plain,
Rise bright before my mental eye
　　When slumber brings a truce to pain,
If these be dreams, I only ask
　　Often to dream such dreams again.

FRANCE.

LAND of my Fathers ! lovely France !
   I greet thee with a glad All hail !
Now thou hast dropped the shattered lance
   And làid aside the glittering mail.
Thy hand the oriflamme has furled,
   Thy voice made war's wild trumpet cease,
And now the whole admiring world
   Has crowned thee Queen of Peace.

In savage conflict countless foes
   O'ermatched thee on the battle-plain,
Filled to the brim thy cup of woes
   And vowed thou ne'er should rise again.

But thou hast risen, and to a height
   Ne'er conquered by avenging steel,
Ne'er stormed by war's imposing might
   With roar of drums and cannon's peal.

By peaceful arts, by toiling hands,
  Well hast thou won thy new renown,
And rightly now thy glorious brow
  Is circled by the civic crown,
And men no more behold thy face
  Distorted by a withering frown.

The busy mill, the vine-clad hill,
  The plowshare furrowing the field,
The artist with creative skill
  Pencil and chisel trained to wield

These rally to thee every heart,
  That loves the Beautiful and True;
We kneel before thee Queen of Art,
  With homage justly true.

Peaceful, but armed, should foreign guns
  Again thy noble breast assail,
Against the valor of thy sons
  Numbers would not avail.

Bitter the lesson thou hast learned,
  Thy taskmaster a ruthless foe;
But truest glory hast thou earned
  Through agony and woe.

And now pursue thy high career,
The world regards thy proud advance
And millions peal the loud acclaim
Of *salut à la France !*

CHRISTIANOS AD LEONES.

GIVE the Christians to the lions ! was the savage Roman
cry,
And the vestal virgins added, their voices shrill and
high,
And Cæsar gave the order : " Loose the lions from their
den !
For Rome must have a spectacle worthy of gods and
men."

Forth to the broad arena a little band was led,
But words forbear to utter how the sinless blood was
shed,
No sigh the victims proffered, but now and then a
prayer,
From lips of age and lips of youth rose upward on the
air ;

And the savage Cæsar muttered : " By Hercules I
  swear,
Braver than gladiators these dogs of Christians are."

Then a lictor bending slavishly, saluting with his axe,
Said, " Mighty Imperator ! the sport one feature lacks ;
We have an Afric lion, savage and great of limb,
Fasting since yestreen. Is the Grecian maid for him ? "

The emperor assented. With a frantic roar and bound,
The monster, bursting from his den, gazed terribly
  around,
And toward him moved a maiden, slowly but yet serene.
" By Venus ! " cried the emperor, " she walketh like a
  queen."

Unconscious of the myriad eyes she crossed the blood-
  soaked sand,
Till face to face the maid and beast, in opposition
  stand ;
The daughter of Athene, in white arrayed and fair,
Gazed on the monster's lowered brow and breathed a
  silent prayer.
Then forth she drew a crucifix and held it high in air.

Lo and behold ! a miracle ! the lion's fury fled,

And at the Christian maiden's feet he laid his lordly
head.

While as she fearlessly caressed, he slowly rose, and
then,

With one soft backward look at her, retreated to his
den.

One shout rose from the multitude, tossed like a stormy
sea ;

" The gods have so decreed it, let the Grecian maid go
free."

Within the Catacombs that night, a saint with snowy
hair,

Folded upon his aged breast his daughter young and
fair ;

And gathered brethren lifted a chant of praise and
prayer :

From the monster of the desert, from the heathen
fierce and wild,

God hath restored to life and love his sinless, trusting
child.

TO MY DEAR NIECE, ROSA B. HUNT.

If in the winter of my life
    I ever could forget its spring,
Thy voice its music would recall,
    Thy smile would back its brightness bring.

So when across the lurid sky
    The clouds in black procession march,
They change to the delighted eye,
    Beneath the rainbow's glowing arch.

And thus the weary traveller,
    Almost despairing of repose,
Limping along the downward path,
    Is gladdened by the way-side rose.

Forgive, I pray, this tuneless lay—
    Words will not come at my command,
And I can only simply say,
    I am thine ever, heart and hand.

SEA-SIDE VISIONS.

ALONG the hard gray beach we strayed,
　　As sunset melted from the sight,
And stars were one by one displayed
　　Upon the azure flag of night—
The breeze came off the misty main,
　　With healing in its balmy breath,
Silent above, the glittering train,
　　Below, the hush of death.

Then buried memories awoke,
　　The phantom glories of the past ;
Voices long hushed, in music spoke
　　To yearning hearts they thrilled at last,
Hands long since mouldered in the dust,
　　Returned a pressure fond and warm ;
Hearts beat again we loved to trust,
　　Through sunshine and through storm.

And thus our unsealed eyes beheld
　　Visions beyond mere mortal scope,
The future life—the buried eld,
　　A memory and a hope.

These mysteries did nature **teach**
 As on we moved with noiseless tread,
And thus upon the starlit beach
 The sea gave **up its** dead.

THE OLD MILL-WHEEL.

THERE'S music in the glen
 Where the bright water tosses,
 As the rocky shelf it crosses,
 With a never-ending **song**
 That the echoing hills prolong,
And give back again and again.
 From the dam on the **hill**
 Pours the white wave **at will,**
 But the old mill-wheel stands still.

There's a rushing in the glen—
 A movement of life
 In the wild water's strife,
 In the tossing of the trees
 In the arms of the breeze
That shakes them again and again.

There's life and there's will
The deep gorge to fill
But the old mill-wheel stands still.

There's sunshine in the glen—
It glitters on the branches,
On the white wave it launches
Like an arrow from the bow,
Or an avalanche of snow
Ever falling, falling, falling—but then
Though the pleasant sunbeams fill
The gorge beneath the hill
Bleak and cold stands the wheel of the mill

It stands a thing apart—
A shadow in the brightness,
A spectre in the lightness,
Amidst the music, dumb ;
In the sunbeams, black and numb ;
Like a sorrow-stricken heart,
That no pulses ever thrill,
That no joys of life can fill,
So the old mill-wheel stands still.

THE SPANISH WRECK.

ANCHORED fast in the yellow sand,
　Like a mammoth skeleton bare to view,
The ribs of the wreck, when the tide is down,
　Their shadows fling to the waters blue.
Streamer, and flag, and woven sail,
　And mast, and yard, there are none to see,
Nor decks to tread, nor helm to guide,
　Nor wealth in foundered argosy.

No one living there is who saw
　The vessel drift to her dreaded fate,
When night hung black on the iron coast,
　And surges roared with a voice of hate.
They are gone who once heard the minute gun
　The tale of peril and woe proclaim,
What time the flag with its union down
　Was shown by the levin and rocket's flame.

Bleaching below in coral caves
　Are they who trod on the gallant deck ;
Vainly aloft the tempest raves,
　They sleep with the gold of the Spanish wreck.

With rusted blades and mouldering guns,
   And caskets of fashion and value **rare** :
The fruit of many a toilsome hour
   And deed of daring is wasted there.

But when the full moon is eclipsed,
   Once in a term of many years,
And the sounding sea is as black as death,
   Strange stir of life in the wreck appears.
Masts shoot up from the deck restored,
   Sheathing glitters along her sides,
Figures move to and fro aboard,
   And lanterns gleam in the shuddering tide.

Manhood is there, and beauty **fair** ;
   The cup is passed from hand to hand,
And bearded lips are dashed with wine,
   And laughter floats on the air to land.
Then a sudden rush of armed men—
   A clash of steel ! a cry of woe !
The vision fades into naught again,
   And rayless the midnight waters flow.

But sorrow betides the luckless wight
 Whoe'er doth the phantom revel see—
 E'er ever a year pass over his head,
  His bed with the drowned of the wreck shall be.
Seek not to fathom these mysteries dark—
 Seek not for visions, but pass thy way—
Nor question the crimes of the sunken bark :
 Let them sleep, let them sleep till the final day.

THE INDIAN SUMMER.

Autumn has come and winter's step is near,
 His footsteps rustle in the falling leaves,
His chill breath murmurs in the herbage sere,
 His frown would darken even the garnered sheaves ;
But kindly nature mitigates his frown,
And gilds the dying year with glories all her own.

Before our raptured senses now unfold
 Scenes of a pageant summer, one more bright,
In varied hues and garniture of gold
 Than "leafy June" e'er offered to the sight.

The sweeping wooded-hills are all ablaze,
And myriad rainbows glimmer through the golden
    haze.

The limpid streams that saunter by,
  A burnished mirror in each tiny wave,
Reward the gaze of the delighted eye ;
   For jewels, such as decked Aladdin's cave,
Shine from their liquid depths in wavering light,
From morn till noon, from noon till dewy night.

And every bright-winged and melodious bird,
  That loves the woodland haunt and sylvan dell,
By the strong spirit of his nature stirred,
  Pours to the parting year his wild farewell.
Alas ! too soon the gorgeous masque must end,
And chilling skies o'er leafless bowers in sadness bend.

How like a monarch regal autumn dies !
  With Tyrian robes and gems his couch is strown ;
Above, the drapery of the golden skies,
  Beneath, the splendors of a matchless throne.
Music to fill with joy the dying ear,
And bear the spirit to a brighter sphere.

9

So died the Sachem, lord of these deep woods,
  Brightly apparelled, in the days of old ;
So lay in state beside the rolling floods,
  Gay with flamingo plumes and clasps of gold ;
And trophies of the battle and the chase,
Smiling on death with unaverted face.

SAUNTAUG LAKE, LYNNFIELD, MASS.

DEEP nestled amid verdant trees,
  That e'en at noon a twilight make,
Scarce ruffled by the passing breeze,
  There lies a solitary lake.
A ruder gust, 'tis true, may curl
  Its dimpled surface now and then ;
But soon subsides the transient whirl
  And all is calm again.

Yet sleep the waters calm and bright,
  Where wavering trees inverted grow,
And many a fathom from the light
  The plummet line will sink below.

So from the garish world concealed,
  Lives some serene and quiet heart,
Its depth of feeling unrevealed,
  A thing alone—apart.

The few who seek may haply find
  Charms that escape the careless eye,
Pulses that thrill to fingers kind,
  Throbs that to kindred throbs reply—
And as the skies their azure hue
  To this sequestered lake impart,
So heaven itself, serene and true,
  Is mirrored in the quiet heart.

A WINTER ROUNDELAY.

WITH gentle step hath winter come,
  As loath to spurn the leaflets sere,
The withered garlands autumn flings
  On summer's melancholy bier.
The gray-beard pauses ere he drops
  The snow-white shroud on Nature's face
Surveys her rigid lineaments,
  And marks their yet surviving grace:

Deal gently with her, sexton cold,

   A moment spare her ere you close

The cere-cloths o'er her lifeless form,

   And leave her to her long repose.

Tears for the last we fain must shed,

   A moment ring the funeral knell

Then—homage to the reigning king,

   And a festal peal from the changful bell!

For the Frosty King of the Northern Pole

Is as merry a king as Old King Cole.

I have called him cold, but his brave frame

With its mail of ice hides a heart of flame.

         Prayers for the dead

         Are so briefly said,

And the tears of mourners are freely shed,

But soon transformed to smiles instead.

'Tis the way of the world, we must take as we find it,

The heart may give laws, but the heart cannot bind it,

   A loyal huzza for the king of the hour,

   A supple knee for the footstool of power!

What are pledges forgotten, and grief for the past,

The Kaiser by right, after all, is the *last*.

Hurrah for King Winter! the king of good cheer—

The Lord of the Seasons, the king of the year!

Sweeping **through** the forest,
  Howls the bitter wind—
Cutting as ingratitude,
  As perjured love **unkind ;**
Shakes **the cottage** casement,
  Rudely enters in,
Smites the shivering cotter
  Through his raiment thin :
Pinches aged eld,
  Freezes bloodless youth :
Like a sworn tormentor
  Enemy of ruth—

To the deathly hearth-stone
  Childish **arms have brought**
Little withered fagots
  Far and hardly sought.
Little feet frost-bitten,
  Track the ice with blood,
To that cottage hearth-stone,
  From the distant wood.

But the fires are bright in the grand old hall,
And the lamps are lit for a festival,

And bright tropic flowers in every room
Exhale their souls in sweet perfume,
And the music times the twinkling feet,
Of the fair who pant in summer heat ;
The wine cup passes and the revellers swear
The world is a world without a care :
Nor a single thought will they fling away,
As they homeward dart in the fur-piled sleigh,
On the tiny-feet that have trod that path,
Or the hearts that have shrunk from the winter's wrath,

But afar, never seen by mortal eyes,
There's a realm in endless light that lies,
More fair than the lord of Italian skies,
Where changeless summer forever beams,
Where a fountain of joy forever streams,
Where music dwells in the very air,
And the spirit of love is every where ;
When the tiny feet will bleed no more,
For soft are the paths of that blessed shore ;
And the heavy cross is left behind,
And amaranth wreaths the temples bind ;
And he who the weariest path has trod,
Will nearest stand to the throne of God.

TO MY DAUGHTER.

On the Anniversary of her Wedding-Day, Oct. 31, 1878.

I NEED not say blest be this **day,**
  For blessings always **wait**
On those whom **truest love unites,**
  " **Equal to either fate.**"
To one all worthy of the gift
  We gave the child we loved,
For we believed him true as steel,
  As time has more than proved.
May flowers arise beside your path,
  'Neath Fortune's favoring breath,
Naught can **two** trusting hearts **divide,**
  Not **even the hand of Death.**

THE BETRAYER.

Suggested by a Picture in the Royal Gallery at Brussels.

Through the hushed midnight from the **city** gates,
Great-eyed with nameless terror comes there **one**
In sordid garb and **disheveled hair,**
Clutching a **purse from** which each step he takes

Echoes the clink of coin—a bait for robbers ;
Sudden he stops—his eyes dilated, mark
Flame-reddened smoke arising from a hollow,
His ears have caught the ring of busy hammers,
Token of human neighborhood, mechanics,
Whose daily bread is earned by daily wage,
The fruits of honest toil. The wayfarer
Moves toward the sound. Then comes a brief demand,
A Roman sentry's challenge, "Who goes there ? "
" A friend." " If so, tell me the name thou bearest."
" *Judas Iscariot.*" The centurion scowled.
" I would not bear that name for all the wealth
Of all the Orient kings. No, naked, rather
Would face the lions in the Flavian circus,
Or make my bed in Etna's crimson gorge."
" What make you here by torchlight ? "
The crouching artisans an opening made,
Disclosing to the wild, enquiring glare
Prone on the earth a monstrous Latin cross.
" To-morrow morn," the stern centurion said,
" That fatal tree will bear its weighty fruit,
We but prepare the cross, you send the victim,
To-night the wood is fair, to-morrow's eve
Will see it dark with blood, each drop of which

Were worth a nation's ransom. Those in power
Drove a sharp bargain with the traitor Judas,
Your God or gods are none of mine, but yet
I hold the prophet we shall slay to-morrow
Guiltless of all offence. What multitudes
Followed his steps and hung upon his lips
As if Apollo's music or the voice
Of Orpheus had touched them !
With a wave of his right hand he might have raised a
          host,
And swayed it like a warrior king, but he,
With all the means of war, still counselled peace
And preached to converts ; so, to-morrow noon
A dozen spears will hold the mob in check."
Then to the traitor's soul appeared at last,
In all its appalling magnitude,
The greatness of his crime. He had betrayed
No man, but all humanity. He saw
Before his glaring eyes the radiant form
Of Him who had been Teacher, Master, *Friend,*
Pierced by relentless steel, ashen in hue,
Yet flecked with drops of blood ; the hands that ever
Opened to give, or else were raised to bless,
Mangled and torn ; the voice that bade young children

Come to his sheltering arms, convulsed with sobs,
Yet breathing with distinct and sweetest music,
Forgiveness to his foes, yea, even to Judas.
But tho' **his** Saviour **could remit his sin,**
Treason could not forgive itself.   He knew
That life for him would be perpetual death ;
That even the leper would reject his alms,
That woman's **love,** foretaste of paradise,
Could ne'er be his, **and forth** into the night
He fled to death.   **Inexorable judge,**
An executioner himself.   His crime
Immeasurably **great, but** impotent,
Like every monstrous evil.

THE WEATHER.

THE weather in these latter days
　　Is really most trying,
One moment **you are shivering,**
　　The next one you are frying.
You go abroad in linen pants
　　In blazing sunshine dying ;

Meanwhile the nimble mercury
　To ninety-nine is flying ;
When lo ! from south to east the wind
　Wears round—how mortifying !
At night beneath a coverlid
　And blankets you are lying.
But ten to one, at 6 A. M.,
　With murderous heat you're sighing,
Or draughts of water dashed with ice
　To cool your fauces plying.
The weather now is tropical
　With that of Borneo vieing
And then again in polar realms,
　Old Boston seems to lie in ;
It's a sorry clime for living in,
But a first rate one to die in.

SONS OF ERIN ! TO THE BATTLE !

Sons of Erin ! to the battle !
　Lo ! the iron die is cast,
Even now the cannon's rattle
　Rises on the ocean's blast.

Years on years of bitter anguish,
    Wasting famine, grinding chain,
Hearts in exile doomed to languish,
    These have not been in vain.

Patient waiting—humble craving—
    How has England paid you back ;
See ! she sends the bloodhounds raving
    Fiery-mouthed upon your track.
Even now the axe is gleaming,
    Gloom the scaffold and the block ;
While the bloody red-cross streaming
    Leads her legions to the shock.

Up then ! men of heart and spirit,
    Worthy sons of fatherland,
Men of Ireland, who inherit
    Gallant souls the test to stand.
Heaven the way to death is lighting,
    Bravely fight and nobly fall,
Better die for freedom fighting,
    Than survive the Saxon's thrall.

Shrink not at the cannon's thunder,

   Quail not at the serried van,

Charge ! and cleave their ranks asunder,

   Give the pike to horse and man.

Rouse ye for the fierce ordeal

   And the patriot's soldier's joy—

In the fiery onslaught be all

   Like the men of Fontenoy.

Sons of Erin ! proudly gazing

   On your deeds the world shall stand,

While your emerald banner blazing

   Sheds a halo round your hand.

Win a noble page in story,

   And the record proud shall be,

Living in immortal glory,

   Ireland fought and she was free !

END.